Ordinary Women Extraordinary Strength

by Barbara Cook

For Barbara

II Cor. 5:15

Barbara Cook

Aglow Publications

A Ministry of Women's Aglow Fellowship, Int'l.
P.O. Box 1548
Lynnwood, WA 98046-1558
USA

To
Jerry Cook
my beloved husband,
best friend, and partner
in the life of grace

Cover design by David Marty

Unless otherwise noted, all scripture quotations in this publication are from the Holy Bible, New International Version. Copyright 1973, 1978, 1984, International Bible Society. Other version is abbreviated as follows: KJV (King James Version).

ISBN 0-932305-55-5

Table of Contents

04 760

Introduction

"Why are we afraid to be strong?" I asked a group of women.

"Because we might be domineering," answered one.

"I think it's really a fear of rejection," said another.

"Men don't like strong women," added a third.

This book answers the real fears of these women. It recognizes our dilemma: We admire strength in others yet tend to have negative attitudes toward strength in ourselves. Within the pages of this book, you will find a model of strength which loses none of the warmth and softness we associate with femininity. This kind of strength never expresses itself in domineering behavior, harshness, coercion, or control of others. This is a book for the *ordinary* woman who desires *extraordinary* strength in order to successfully meet the challenges of her life.

This book is for the capable, ordinary woman who desires more than mere survival and more than a life of self-centered accumulation of things. She wants to use her gifts and talents in service and love. She has the·courage to grow in her personal and spiritual life.

Finally, this book is for the woman who feels weak, tired, helpless, frustrated, or victimized. She is often sad, disappointed, and despondent. Perhaps she struggles with self-destructive addictions or eating disorders.

This book offers, not just temporary relief, nor a few positive thoughts, but a new way to live, a new identity, a stable source of self-worth and confidence. In the pages of this book, you will find basic truths to enable you to live and love courageously, joyously, and at peace with yourself.

Chapter 1

Can a Woman be Strong?

I spent a large portion of my childhood swinging from tall trees. Few girls lived in the neighborhood, so my playmates were boys.

Tarzan stories inspired one of the older boys to construct a network of long ropes for us to swing from tree to tree. Over the years, we hauled lumber scraps high into the oaks and maples to build tree houses, forts, and even ammunition storage depots.

Our ammunition: black walnuts stored in coffee cans nailed to the trees. We bombed enemy invaders and aliens quite efficiently, sending them screaming out of our turf.

One afternoon when I was alone in the woods checking the ammo supplies, I heard the voices of invaders below.

"Wonder whose fort this is?" one asked.

"Barbara and her gang's. I hear she beat up Tim Kelley."

"She did? Let's get outa here!"

When I learned how to play paper dolls and "house," those pursuits seemed dull in contrast to the more adventuresome life I'd lived.

If my mother worried whether her daughter would ever grow into a lady, she never expressed it. When my grandmother complained, Mother defended my right to my own interests. She insisted she was happy to have such a strong, healthy child.

Adolescence changed my relationships considerably when it came to boys. I stopped beating up Tim Kelley and gave up walnut wars for new interests like fashion, makeup, sewing, and even a little cooking. If my parents had harbored secret worries about their tomboy daughter, those concerns were now traded in on discussions of rules for dating.

But adolescence did nothing to change the adventuresome habits I'd developed. With the boys, I continued to dive off high bridges into deep water, chase snakes, collect spiders, and shoot 22's.

Many years later, I discovered the error of my ways from a book. "Men don't like women who kill their own snakes," the writer observed. "Women are made to be soft and feminine. They need to be taken care of."

A quick check assured me I was indeed soft. But now a subtle doubt arose—"Maybe I'm not feminine."

Many of us identify with this dilemma. A part of us abhors the idea of pretending to be helpless, denying our own strength. But another part loves being a woman and draws up in fear at any suggestion of losing femininity.

Here's the good news: God doesn't intend to leave us in inner conflict.

Strong is not often considered a feminine adjective. When associated with women, it often carries a negative connotation—like the loudmouthed, red-faced females who wield rolling pins and throw plates when angry. A woman who "comes on strong" is out to catch, dominate, or control. She is too forward, too frank, too harsh, or too brassy. In the office, she's the person who readily gives her opinion. She's the wife who nags, the bossy school teacher, the matronly head of affairs in the local church. Her capabilities are great, but...

Influenced by these images, I feared my strength. "Hold it down, Barbara," I told myself. "People won't like you. You'll become dominating, overbearing. Try to be weak. Pretend you are a soft, delicate flower."

The Bible doesn't qualify strong, though. It says quite bluntly:

"Be *strong* and courageous" (Josh. 1:6).

"But the people that do know their God shall be *strong* and do *exploits*" (Dan. 11:32 KJV).

"Be *strengthened* with might by his Spirit in the inner man"(Eph. 3:16 KJV). (Italics mine.)

I wondered about those verses. Did this mean *me?* Or were the verses on strength written only to men? As I study the Bible, I find much to encourage personal strength in me as a child of God.

Contradicting this is an image of femininity held by many Christians which suggests that a truly godly woman is always passive, sweet, gentle, soft, quiet, meek, and submissive. A truly godly man, on the other hand, is strong, assertive, bold, courageous, and dominant.

For example, many youth pastors and camp speakers exhort teens to be "ladies and gentlemen," to learn their proper roles. 1 John 2:14 is a popular text for use with the young men:

"I write to you, young men, because you are strong, and the word of God lives in you, and you have overcome the evil one."

The speaker may say something to this effect: "It's natural for you young men to want to be strong, to become *real men*. These fine young Christian women admire a man's man. They want to marry a strong, masculine man, not some sissy. Jesus Christ was a real man. He was strong. And God wants you to be a real man, someone strong."

The young women gain the impression that strength and masculinity are synonymous. Rarely does a speaker include in one of these "ladies and gentlemen" messages any encouragement for women to be strong.

STRONG WOMEN IN THE BIBLE

We read in the Bible of strong and mighty men. Jesus was a man of strong personality. David, Paul, Stephen, and Peter are familiar figures of strength. Because of an emphasis on strong men, we sometimes overlook the mighty women in the Bible, but they are there: Priscilla, Phoebe, and Sarah. Or Miriam, Deborah, Huldah, Esther, and Abigail.

These were not quiet, retiring ladies who never let their thoughts be known. They did not wait to respond to action; they created the action. If God created women to be responders rather than initiators, these women hadn't heard about it.

THE VIRTUOUS WOMAN

The Proverbs 31 woman is sometimes called "God's ideal woman," but we can't assume that she *alone* represents the ideal. Nor do we believe she is meant to be a rigid pattern for the daily activities of our lives. If she were, today's woman would have to grow wool and flax, spin yarn, weave fabric, dye it, and then sew clothing fit for royalty.

Proverbs 31 has been the text of hundreds of Mother's Day sermons. Many women have shared with me their feelings of guilt and discouragement after such sermons. And some feel like Trish, who said, "It makes me tired just to read Proverbs 31. I've decided to skip that part of the Bible from now on."

Certainly that was not God's purpose. Neither was he trying to tell us we should all become superwomen or model homemakers, decorators, gourmet cooks, and seamstresses. No. God gave the virtuous woman to us as a sample, the sort of person he commends, a role model of what we can be.

This illustrative woman is pictured in many different phases of life and in varied spheres of activity. She valued her home but was not imprisoned in it. She involved herself in the world of business, took an interest in the poor of her community, and still found time to enjoy life. She was neither selfish nor a martyr, neither materialist nor superspiritual.

In a Bible study, we once listed the character traits we saw in the Proverbs woman. She was:

caring	*confident*	*creative*
diligent	*discreet*	*enterprising*
enthusiastic	*generous*	*hopeful*
hospitable	*joyful*	*kind*

Ordinary Women—Extraordinary Strength

loving	*loyal*	*resourceful*
respectful	*secure*	*strong*
trustworthy	*serving*	*wise*

The Hebrew word translated "virtuous" in the King James Version and "noble" in the New International Version (vv. 10,29) was a commonly used word, *chayil*. In order to understand what the writer had in mind, look at how else it was used. Generally chosen to describe not saintly women but strong men, *chayil* is often translated strength, valiant, might, or fighting. For example:

"You armed me with *strength* (chayil) for battle; you made my adversaries bow at my feet" (2 Sam. 22:40).

"It is God who arms me with *strength* (chayil) and makes my way perfect" (Ps. 18:32).

"You armed me with *strength* (chayil) for battle" (Ps. 18:39).

"The king of Babylon also deported to Babylon the entire force of seven thousand fighting men, *strong* (chayil) and fit for war" (2 Kings 24:16).

"The relatives who were *fighting* (chayil) men...were 87,000 in all" (1 Chron. 7:5).

"*Valiant* (chayil) men lie plundered" (Ps. 76:5).

"'Not by *might* (chayil) nor by power, but by my Spirit,' says the Lord Almighty" (Zech. 4:6). (Italics mine.)

The Hebrews used this word to describe someone powerful. In fact, we could most accurately entitle the woman of Proverbs 31 "the mighty woman," "the valiant woman," or "the woman of strength and power." In keeping with the whole of Scripture, we see pictured here a person who *understands the source of strength*.

Also, this woman exemplified what we call the "fruit of

the Spirit." Note the character traits found in Galatians 5:22.

"But the fruit of the Spirit is love, joy, peace, patience, kindness, goodness, faithfulness, gentleness and self-control."

Some of her skills and abilities also compare to the manifestations of the Holy Spirit listed in 1 Corinthians 12:7-10:

Now to each one the manifestation of the Spirit is given for the common good. To one there is given through the Spirit the message of wisdom, to another the message of knowledge by means of the same Spirit, to another faith by the same Spirit, to another gifts of healing by that one Spirit, to another miraculous powers, to another prophecy, to another the ability to distinguish between spirits, to another the ability to speak in different kinds of tongues, and to still another the interpretation of tongues.

These are sometimes called "the gifts of the Spirit" as are also the gifts (*charismata*) listed in Romans 12:6-8. Again, notice the similarities:

We have different gifts, according to the grace given us. If a man's gift is prophesying, let him use it in proportion to his faith. If it is serving, let him serve; if it is teaching, let him teach; if it is encouraging, let him encourage; if it is contributing to the needs of others, let him give generously; if it is leadership, let him govern diligently; if it is showing mercy, let him do it cheerfully.

Here, Christians are described as expressing love through

17

their ability to serve (who works with eager hands), to give money with generosity (stretching out her arms to the poor and needy), to lead (she speaks with wisdom), to encourage (she watches over the affairs of her household), to teach (faithful teaching is on her tongue). Romans 12 is one of many biblical portraits of mature godliness. Proverbs 31 contains another such portrait—a portrait of a woman clothed with strength and dignity.

A consistent view of strength is presented throughout the Bible. True strength includes both character traits and abilities derived from a relationship with God. True strength, true might, true ability to serve others and express the image of God all come from a Source other than ourselves. They emerge out of a life joined to its Creator.

Some women who *seem* strong may also seem obnoxious or masculine or domineering. If strong denotes a person who is officious, commandeering, egotistical, or selfish, then her kind of strength is unacceptable. Those qualities arise from weakness, not strength. But if strong refers to a personality of substance or influence, then we want to be women of strength—fully living life to the glory of God.

STRENGTH IS NOT CONTROL

To confuse strength with control or domination is a mistake. The Bible's comments on strength and authority should never be misconstrued to justify domination, exploitation, owner-ship, or control of other people. In fact, authoritarian forms of leadership are forbidden to Christians:

Jesus called them together and said, "You know that those who are regarded as rulers of the Gentiles *lord it over them* and their high officials exercise *authority over them.* Not so with you. Instead, whoever wants to become great among you must be your servant, and whoever wants to be first must be slave of all" (Mark 10:42-45). (Italics mine.)

This directive applies to all relationships, allowing them to be rich and fulfilling. Thus, in relating to men, we have no need for games or competition. We are free to enjoy genuine mature love. We are free to build a healthy marriage. When we know our strength comes from God, we have no need to control others. We know our power is for serving, giving, and loving.

STRENGTH DOES NOT DOMINATE

Christian strength doesn't seek to dominate, to coerce, to compete, or to prove something. True strength is not arrogant or pushy, nor does it work to establish an identity. Rather, it flows freely from the woman who possesses a sense of identity.

Rather than demanding love, this strength issues from an experience of *being* loved; and it is unafraid to say, "I love you. Can I help?" It is equally unafraid to say, "I need you. Can you help me?" It delights in giving, accepting, forgiving, enduring.

The Bible is packed full of information on strength, defining strength as God sees it. God's word repeatedly commands us to be strong, even in the face of impossibilities. The Bible encourages us to possess strength, to *live* in strength, and to *be* strengthening persons in our relations with others. No picture is painted on the pages of Scripture of women who, in the name of their God, pretended weakness or feigned helplessness in order to be feminine.

Ordinary Women—Extraordinary Strength

The Bible doesn't once exhort women to be passive, to lie down and be walked on, to allow themselves to be victimized, exploited, or used. Instead, it tells the stories of women who found the Source of strength and had the courage to use it. Women like this didn't go out with the Old Testament. Many women of strength are alive and well in the church today.

Consider Aida Skripnikova, a Christian in Russia:

For distributing on the streets of Leningrad a poem she had composed that ended with the line, "Seek God while He is to be found," Aida was arrested and lost her job and the right to live in Leningrad. This young woman courageously continued to proclaim her faith in spite of prison sentences and psychiatric "treatments." Attacked by numerous articles in the Soviet press, she wrote powerful replies that, of course, the government press refused to print—antireligious propaganda is allowed but not religious propaganda—but public curiosity was aroused about this girl, people wanted to know what she had done and what she had written, and handwritten copies of her replies to these articles were circulated throughout Russia.[1]

She asked this question: Would you be content to discuss theater only in a theater, or sports only in a stadium? Then why must a Christian only be allowed to speak of God in a church? You can gather with your friends at any time to speak on any subject, but a Christian breaks the law if he visits a friend and they talk of Jesus Christ who is life itself to them. Is this just?[2]

Aida's example and that of many other courageous women behind the iron curtain prove biblical strength is not a myth.

And it's more than a positive mental attitude or a healthy self-image.

This is the power which doesn't disappear when the pressure's on. More than political power and more than financial power, it's a sure and steady might on the inside—fueled from a Source greater than either mortal mind or muscular conditioning.

If we women discover this kind of power, we will lose interest in all the destructive deadends we have pursued before. We will no longer tolerate abuse against our bodies or persons. We will gladly give up the manipulative and seductive games played in hopes of increasing our power. We will behave as adults, happily abandoning little-girl coyness and sulking, along with little-girl dependencies and resentments.

Women who hate men need this power to transform their relationships. Women who love men too much need this strength in order to give up their victimized habits. Women who desire to be godly need this strength to achieve their goal. We all need this power.

If women knew—really knew—of the strength and power available to them in Christ, they would rush into his kingdom en masse. It should be no well kept secret. It must be proclaimed daily in the lives of those who have discovered it.

Ordinary Women—Extraordinary Strength

FOR YOUR OWN BIBLE STUDY

Strength and Power

Joshua 1:6, 9,10	2 Corinthians 12:9,10
Proverbs 31:17	Ephesians 3:16
Psalm 18:32	Ephesians 6:10
Psalm 27:14	Colossians 1:11
Isaiah 40:31	Philippians 4:13

Strong Women in the Bible

Sarah: Genesis 16,17; Hebrews 11:11

Miriam: Exodus 15:20,21

Deborah: Judges 4,5

Abigail: 1 Samuel 25

Huldah: 2 Kings 22; 2 Chronicles 34

Esther: Book of Esther

Mary, Martha: Luke 10:38-41; John 11:1-44

Priscilla: Acts 18:1-3,18,19,24-26

Chapter 2

What Can a Woman Be?

Can we women be intelligent as well as strong? How intelligent can we be? How smart is too smart? How capable is too capable? Are boundaries set on our desires, talents, and abilities? Which inner aspirations are from God? Which desires, goals, and dreams are reasonable and right? What is our potential for giving, loving, and achieving? What are God's intentions for us?

These are important questions. Our attitudes toward strength will shape our answers. And conversely, our answers will shape our views of our own strength because these sensitive subjects relate to our femininity or our view of ourselves as women.

Let's look at our own beliefs about women and examine

the limits we tend to place on a person simply because she is a woman. Are those limits reasonable? Or are they based on the fear of losing something? For example, are the limits we set on our own growth, intelligence, or strength based on a fear that we may lose love? security?

FEAR OF SUCCESS

In her book, *The Cinderella Complex,* Colette Dowling examines the "fear of success" syndrome, showing how pervasively it influences women in our society. Women with outstanding intelligence, ability, and talent who enter business or professions enjoy the rewards of achievement only to a point. When success is about to become theirs, they stop, paralyzed by an unknown fear. In place of excitement, delight, or joy, they feel anxiety. They back off and abandon the gains they worked so hard to achieve.

This fear of success is tied to the notion that a woman must be Cinderella if she is to be loved. Unless she needs rescuing, no prince can come and rescue her. Unless she is a dependent person, in need of someone to take care of her, she will be rejected by men. Where did this fear come from? Is it rational? true?

No. It's one of many subconscious attitudes which influence the limits we set on ourselves. When these unexamined, unfounded attitudes tangle with our notions of God, they become more powerful. We can build a small world for ourselves if we imagine a God who sets narrow boundaries on all persons labeled female. Meanwhile, God is opening the doors of that small world. He is attempting to speak to us of our God-given strength and the opportunities for a full, abundant life that await us.

If, in response to his direction, we can settle any doubts

we may have about the limits set on women, the doors will open wide into a world where our strength finds expression in a variety of ways. Rather than expend our energies to avoid or deny our strength, we can release its power to impact our personal growth both spiritually and mentally. That strength can be expressed rather than camouflaged and hidden behind a facade of fragility.

AFRAID TO WIN

Athletics never came easy for me. Although my childhood in "the woods" was active and physically strenuous, it didn't follow that I excelled when it came to sports. Except for one: Ping-Pong.

My father and I learned Ping-Pong together when I was in my early teens. Throughout my high school years, we played almost daily with each other and anyone else who visited our home.

My growing skill introduced a new dilemma. Most of the players who could provide interesting competition were boys. The unspoken rule was that, if a girl wanted a boy to like her, she must never beat him in a sport. I found myself reluctant to play my best if the fellow at the other end of the table was one I might like to date.

Some girls didn't question that rule. But I liked to play hard and give the competition my best game, win or lose. It felt dishonest to "let" someone win just because he was male.

When I arrived at college in Seattle as a freshman, I discovered a Ping-Pong table where I could always find someone needing a break from study. One night I won a game against a fellow named Jack, who walked out after the defeat looking shaken.

Later I heard that Jack went right home and told his roommate, "I was beaten by a girl."

"You were? Who was she?" asked the roommate.

"She's new. A Barbara Paulson."

Because of this and whatever else Jack may have said, the roommate made up his mind to meet this girl. The roommate was Jerry Cook, now my husband.

SEEING THE BARRIERS

To help us examine our beliefs about femininity and strength, let's reflect on the barriers we run up against when we walk out that newly opened doorway and express the strength God has placed inside us. Many are self-induced, but well-entrenched, barriers which come down slowly and only with careful, thoughtful choices.

Movements have come and gone to liberate us women, to fulfill us, to make us more fascinating, more beautiful, more sexy, more total, and more feminine. Organizations have been formed to keep us "in our place," or to set us on a pedestal, and even some to worship us as revived Greek goddesses. "Women's Role in the Church" is a common seminary course. Theologians speculate as to whether women should be ordained.

Most of these activities result in creating stereotypes which form artificial boundaries and limit our vision of reality.

Let's look at one of the strongest stereotypes: Pastors are always male.

As a youth pastor, I attended a large interdenominational conference. Pastors, collegians, and Christian workers met for four days of study and sharing. I discovered firsthand how ministry might be if I were not married. My badge identified me as "Rev. Barbara Cook," not "wife of Jerry Cook."

With enthusiasm, I headed daily for the special pastors'

class. About four hundred attended; youth pastors, assistant pastors, and senior pastors of small and large churches. *Well, I thought at the first session, a few other women are here. I shouldn't be too conspicuous.* Probably twenty ladies were in the group; but it quickly became apparent they were "wives," not pastors.

Normally I find it easy to make friends in a new group. But this proved to be a rather lonely time.

"Is this seat taken?"

"Uh...yes. I'm saving it for my friend."

As the seats filled up, some unfortunate pastor would end up sitting beside me and politely ask, "Who's your husband?"

When I'd say he wasn't present, the man would make sure he talked only with the men around me. I understood. His reputation was important, and I was not a safe conversation. My badge identified me as a professional peer. But his tradition didn't list me in its dictionary.

The teacher of that pastoral Bible study seemed like a fair-minded scholar. Nevertheless, he addressed his remarks to "we men called of God" and "brothers." Apparently the experience of relating to a woman minister was either new to most of these men or offensive.

The last day, a pastor who had read our books introduced himself, asked my name, and then, "Jerry Cook's wife? Really!"

Within moments, life changed. I had instant friends. The speaker hastened to introduce his wife. Young pastors approached me to ask if a staff opening might come up at our church. *Fun experience,* I thought with a chuckle in my smile. *I'm glad it was four days before they found out whose wife I am.*

29

Ordinary Women—Extraordinary Strength

I am describing a common experience where our stereotypes block us from seeing reality. Something about stereotypes seems inhuman and often contradicts our own knowledge of ourselves. Isn't each of us a unique individual, carefully made in the image of God? Isn't each a custom-made, one-of-a-kind person?

Other barriers we face include:

"Women are emotionally weak."

"Women are more spiritually sensitive."

"Women are subjective."

"Women tend to be indecisive."

"Women belong in the home."

"Women should adapt to their husbands."

"Women are vulnerable to satanic attack."

"Women are gullible."

What about these cliches? Are they tradition or truth, opinion or fact? If true, are they true of *all* women or only of *some* women?

Are these stereotypes only true for those women who believe them? *Should* they be true of Christian women? Is this God's plan?

Does the work of Jesus Christ have any implications for the character traits of women? Does the new birth change our person at its very core? If so, do these changes affect women as thoroughly as they affect men? Does a woman have the right to view herself in a new way when she comes into relationship with Christ? Or must she guard the qualities labeled "feminine"?

Our stereotypes of men are also invalid. We are told:

"Men are strong."

"Men are brave."

"Men are tough, bold, and goal oriented."

"Men are aggressive."

"Men are decisive."

"Men don't cry."

Many marriage courses teach women about the male nature so they can better adjust to it. Some teach that men have stronger sexual desires than women, that men have sensitive egos, that men have difficulty being "wrong."

Supposedly men are turned off by women who:

think independently

have a different opinion

are known to be intelligent

fill a leadership role in a group

beat them in a sport.

Around the world, certain personality traits are identified as "feminine" or "masculine." What is "feminine" differs according to the continent and culture.

POPULAR OPINION POLL

In a group of single Christians, we took a poll asking, "Which of these qualities do you believe are more masculine, which more feminine, and which common to both sexes?"

Qualities such as decisiveness, bravery, security, and tenderness were listed for the secret "ballot." Unknown to the group, we included each fruit of the Spirit from Galatians 5 in the list.

When we tallied results, we discovered nearly all the fruit of the Spirit were considered "feminine" qualities by a large majority. According to this poll, Jesus Christ would not qualify as masculine.

We limit ourselves by accepting stereotypes or roles or someone else's definitions of who we are. How can we become

31

the women God created us to be if we are locked into a preconceived pattern? If the fruit of the Spirit is feminine, does that mean a man becomes less masculine as the Spirit works in him? Or are our definitions wrong?

Could it be that *both* men and women can grow into the potential for which they were created as they allow God to work? The fruit of new life in Christ is wholeness of personality. Jesus is our example. He showed us what wholeness looks like. He displayed the character traits we all want in our lives, whether we are male or female.

At times, Jesus behaved in ways that Americans have traditionally called feminine: Jesus showed his emotions, even wept while the public watched. He evidenced "motherly" feelings as he exclaimed, "O Jerusalem, Jerusalem...how often I have longed to gather your children together, as a hen gathers her chicks under her wings" (Luke 13:34).

Jesus also demonstrated behavior traditionally labelled male: the assertive, angry cleansing of the temple; the protective concern he showed for his mother just before he died; and the commanding manner in which he preached and taught.

Some sort of unisex is not the answer. If that were possible (which it isn't), it would lead to an exceedingly boring world. Rather, let's examine our *assumptions* about femininity. If our definitions of femininity block our allowing the Lord to change us, the definitions are wrong. If "feminine" is an imprisoning term to us, we must compare our definitions to the Bible's standards and form new, biblical premises.

We raise many questions when we ask "What can a woman be?" As we examine Scripture, let's ask ourselves:

Which women were especially effective in God's purposes?

Which were chosen for special tasks or honor?

Which did God describe as examples of godliness?

What qualities did God name as admirable in women?

How do these qualities square with our notions of femininity?

This chapter is packed full of questions. More questions than answers, in fact. That is deliberate. I am purposely raising questions which will stimulate us to take a long look at our belief system regarding women. What can a woman be? is a question we must face, for our answer dictates our decisions and attitudes regarding strength in women.

To hear what the Scripture offers women as sources of strength and power, we must challenge all the limits we may have placed on ourselves. We must eradicate the mental blocks, preconceptions, and subtle stereotypes which allow us to read incredible passages of scriptural truth and relegate them to men, turning away from the personal power they promise us.

We must also raise the ceiling on our definitions of ourselves and other women. If we seek with open minds, we'll find an exciting answer to the query, How strong can a woman be?

We will discover what it means to be strong and, at the same time, feminine. We will develop a powerful sense of identity, strong self-worth, internal security, and self-confidence. We will see how beautifully the word of God supplies strength for every need.

We must begin, of course, at the beginning. We begin not with who we hope to be some day, but with the person we are now.

Chapter 3

Strength in Identity

We women too often dwell on who we are not, what we *ought* to be, what kind of wives we should be, what kind of mothers we should have been (and have failed to be), or what kind of Christians we wish we were.

In focusing on who we are not, we forfeit learning who we are; that is, who God says we are. We obscure our true identity or worse yet, never discover it. The Scriptures tell us our identity is in Christ. He is the source of an identity based on reality, an identity already given us.

This positive identity is one of our sources of strength. Discovering it can eliminate forever the struggle to achieve identity which depletes large amounts of our energy. When we know who we are, we can live confidently.

A NEW BASE FOR IDENTITY

Accepted norms for identity vary from country to country. In some places, a girl's identity is fixed at birth—based upon the family into which she is born.

In another place or another time, identity may be based on a child's looks, physical strength or handicaps, attractiveness, or unattractiveness. Qualities over which a child has no control become the basis for her identity. Though unfair, it is practiced to some extent in every nation.

Americans prematurely fit the identities of children into such categories as "bright," "beautiful," "talented," or "athletic." We see the effects of this in the post-college athlete struggling to find identity after football or an insecure aging woman once known as beautiful. Still, few question this labeling practice. We tend to accept it as "the way things are."

As believers, we must guard against the error of believing that "what is" is the way it should be. Christians have an entirely new basis for identity. This new basis is a foundational reality which transcends any culture's evaluation of a person. "What is" should be evaluated by God's revelation.

NARROW BOXES

Any basis for identity set down by humans is not adequate for a lifetime. It provides too narrow a definition, too miniature a base on which to build a real person. Our world's foundations for identity are far too limiting, too constricting. They may be useful to society, but they can be detrimental to us as individuals. A narrow box does not give us the identity necessary to express the real strength inside. We need a large base for identity to release our strength.

Even the church falls into a limiting pattern. Christians expect identity through a position in a group. "I am an elder."

"I have the gift of prophecy." Or, "I am the leader of our women's group." "I'm a board member." Roles are fleeting and changeable. Positions do not tell us who we are; they are not a sufficient base for a strong identity.

If asked to tell someone who you are, you could give yourself many descriptions—many definitions of identity—wife, mother, or single person. You could describe your identity in terms of career, achievements, intelligence, physical appearance, or race. But to find a more lasting, dependable basis for identity, these must be laid aside as you ask, "How does God define me?"

THE IN-CHRIST PEOPLE

Who does God say we are?

As we look in the Scriptures, we'll notice something exciting: The New Testament writers used far more words to tell believers who they are than to tell them who they are not. Repeatedly they encourage the saints to know who they are *in Christ;* to know they are people of hope, people brought out of darkness into light, heirs of salvation, priests and kings unto God...the list goes on and on. To discover the true elements of our identity, a serious reading of the New Testament is a must. As we read, awareness of our true strength will grow.

Ephesians is a good place to start; it makes frequent use of the terms "in him" and "in Christ." It reiterates, "in Christ you are..." or "you have..." or "in him you have been made..." Read Ephesians and circle the phrases referring to who you are *in Jesus Christ.* Take note of all the wonderful things God says about you in the first chapter. God wants us to believe what he *really* thinks of us—regardless of what we think of ourselves.

In my own examination of Ephesians, I noticed fourteen phrases like "in Christ" or "in him" or "in the Lord." For instance, it says, "you are light *in the Lord*" (Eph. 5:8), "be strong *in the Lord* and in his mighty power" (Eph. 6:10), and also "for he chose us *in him* before the creation of the world to be holy and blameless in his sight" (Eph. 1:4). *"In him* we have redemption through his blood, the forgiveness of sins, in accordance with the riches of God's grace" (Eph. 1:7).

My search for all the "in hims" in the New Testament became a fascinating study. In Philippians, five references are made to "in Christ" or "in him." Colossians tells us eight times what it means to be "in him." First Thessalonians mentions it five times. In First John, I counted twenty-one references to "in Christ."

I began to see that the early Christians thought of themselves as the "in-Christ" people. Being in Christ was basic to their identity, to their power, to their strength.

MARKING OUR BIBLES

Following is a sample of this kind of study. You can use it for any New Testament book from Romans to Revelation.

We need to suspend our preconceived definitions of identity and consider what God says about our true person in the passage we study. Take note of the frequency of "in him" or "in Christ." (In our Bibles, we'd circle those phrases—here I've italicized them.)

Praise be to the God and Father of our Lord Jesus Christ, who has blessed us in the heavenly realms with every spiritual blessing *in Christ*.

For he chose us *in him* before the creation of the world to be holy and blameless in his sight. In love he predestined us to be adopted as his sons *through Jesus Christ,* in accordance with his pleasure and will—to the praise of his glorious grace, which he has freely given us *in the One he loves.*

In him we have redemption through his blood, the forgiveness of sins, in accordance with the riches of God's grace that he lavished on us with all wisdom and understanding. And he made known to us the mystery of his will according to his good pleasure, which he pur- posed *in Christ,* to be put into effect when the times will have reached their fulfillment—to bring all things in heaven and on earth together under one head, even Christ.

In him we were also chosen, having been predestined according to the plan of him who works out everything in conformity with the purpose of his will, in order that we, who were the first to hope *in Christ,* might be for the praise of his glory.

And you also were included *in Christ* when you heard the word of truth, the gospel of your salvation. Having believed, you were marked *in him* with a seal, the prom- ised Holy Spirit, who is a deposit guaranteeing our in- heritance until the redemption of those who are God's possession—to the praise of his glory (Eph. 1:3-14).

Right now, we are heirs to *all* God's promises. Not some- day in the future, not when we make ourselves good enough or perfect enough, but we possess them now because we are *in Jesus Christ.* We are his adopted children. We are beloved and we are accepted in his kingdom. Knowing that can solve a lot of problems and become the internal source of a large measure of personal strength. Believing these facts is a beginning point of living in the strength God has given us.

WHAT ABOUT OUR PAST?

Another important facet of biblical identity is related to the past. Perhaps past experiences shaped our self-concept in negative, crippling ways. On the other hand, they may have shaped us in positive, confident ways. Either way, their effects are no longer the *essence* of our true identity.

Paul says in Galatians 2:20:

"I have been crucified with Christ and I no longer live, but Christ lives in me. The life I live in the body, I live by faith in the Son of God, who loved me and gave himself for me."

Paul's statement is not a declaration of negatives, but of positive truth that the old identity, the one full of sin, independence, and the inability to please God—that person died. We vicariously died with Jesus on the cross. And, not only did we die with him, we rose with him when he emerged from the tomb. The old identity died. The new creation rose with Christ to new life.

Although the life you now live looks like that of an ordinary human being, there's more to you than meets the eye. Because not *only* does an ordinary human being live in your body, the Holy Spirit also lives in you. So, when others see you living a natural human life on this earth, they may think you're only a collection of blood and flesh, bones, and personality. Actually, you are a *redeemed* piece of blood, flesh, bones, and personality. The Spirit living in you can accomplish things that you, in your human limitation, could never do.

We may look like normal human beings, but much more is going on. That's how God sees us. He doesn't see us as failures or successes or as people full of regrets and blunders. He's not trying out the power of positive thinking to see if it will work. Nor is he hoping to produce change in us by positive reinforcement and affirmation. He sees us as re-deemed children of God, full of the Holy Spirit's abundant life. And God is not fooling himself. He sees us as we are, not as he wishes we would be. The same dynamic Holy Spirit indwells every believer. Each man and woman of the "in-Christ" family possesses a new life source; a new dimen-sion of power and ability. Divinely sparked growth is in process.

IN THE SPIRIT

After a week full of seeming failures, I read through Romans 7 and 8 and wondered, *Am I the kind of carnal Chris-tian who walks in the flesh or do I walk in the Spirit?* I was unsure at the moment which more accurately described me. Then I read the phrase, "Ye are not in the flesh, but in the Spirit, if so be that the Spirit of God dwell in you" (KJV). Present tense!

Could it be true? If it were and God was saying, "This is the way it is," then I would be smart to agree with him. I read it again. I began writing, for my own benefit, this descrip-tion of who I am. You can use it as a guide when you study on your own. My thoughts include pieces of many passages beginning with John 15 when Jesus began to describe who *he* thought we are. He said, "I am the vine; you are the branches."

I am in Jesus, the Vine. I am a branch that abides in him, bears fruit, and is pruned from time to time. The fruit of his Spirit grows in me, blooms, matures,

43

and nourishes others with the food of love, joy, peace, longsuffering, gentleness, goodness, faithfulness, kindness, and self-control.

I am *not* in the flesh but in the Spirit. My spirit has resurrected, is raised up to rule with Christ, and is seated in heavenly places with him.

I am a person who has the ability to walk by the Spirit. I am able to make choices which are in line with my eternal destiny: choices that build my person, my character, and my integrity. I can make rational decisions as to how my human appetites, desires, talents, and gifts will be used in furthering God's purposes.

As a new creature in Christ, I am not crippled by any past sins or past choices. They do not represent the measure of who I am. I am a person whose true desire, whether I feel it or not, is to walk by the Spirit and abide in Christ. At the center of my being, I love God and am committed to him. I need not categorize myself by the times I fail to act out my true desires and commitments. The exceptions are not my identity. New creation—that is my identity!

UNREAL IDENTITIES

Whether or not we see ourselves as new creatures becomes obvious in our conversations. When asked who we are, we tell about mistakes: "I'm a divorcee or an overeater or an ex-convict. Well, you see, I married young—it was a bad marriage..." People identify themselves by explaining past tragedies.

Not only do we reinforce our own crippling self-view in this way, we seem adept at helping others into the same false categories. For example, it's convenient to refer to members of a congregation by something notable from their past: "You know Debbie, the one who used to be a prostitute?" Or, "that brother over there, I can't remember his name, the guy who was an alcoholic—you know who I mean?"

A child of God is not an "ex" anything. The emphasis is not on our past, not even as sinners saved by grace. The emphasis is on the present. I have two choices. Either I choose to believe that I am *now* who God says I am, or I declare God is, at best, a hopeless idealist or, at worst, a liar and deceiver. (I may not say this aloud, but my actions and attitudes will reveal what I believe.)

WHEN CHRISTIANS SIN

Is sin no longer an issue for the Christian? If we are in Christ, does it matter if we sin? God's grace covers it. He forgives us and keeps on loving us. Our identity remains intact, so sin doesn't matter.

Quite the contrary! Sin *is* an issue for the Christian—not because we lose God's love, but for deeper, more valid reasons. When I sin, I act in a way that is untrue to myself. It isn't just that I disobey some arbitrary rule; it's that I am acting contrary to my own best interests and contrary to my own true nature. Sin is harmful either to me, this valuable person whom God loves or to another valued human being. It is not the "natural" way for this new creation to live.

Our *identity* is as secure as Christ's finished work on the cross. But we can't ignore the growth process. The Holy Spirit leads us into knowledge and truth. Gradually our thoughts, words, and deeds begin to reflect the inner life of our new creation.

It would be unrealistic to claim that Christians don't sin. We do. But a Christian makes a miserable sinner. Our sins and failures feel painful because they contradict who we are. Sin is contrary to our true nature and the deepest longings of our heart.

HOW ARE CHRISTIANS DIFFERENT?

In one sense, we are sinners like those who do not yet know Christ. That is, we do not always live as we were designed to live. At times, our behavior denies that we're valuable persons, made in the image of God. We act selfishly or independently of God. We make poor choices. We have days where we don't meet our own ideals for behavior...maybe not even as well as does an atheist who happens to excel in self-discipline.

But this must not be the basis for evaluating our growth. Nor is it the foundation of our identity. The difference between us and the unbeliever is that we have responded to God's grace. We are partakers of a new nature. Righteousness is being worked out *in us*. "For it is God who works in you to will and to act according to his good purpose" (Phil. 2:13). This process is not self-discipline, positive thinking, or even will power. The Holy Spirit is at work.

GROWING

The Bible calls our growth "renewing of the mind" or "growing in the grace and knowledge of our Lord Jesus Christ." During the growth process, we can expect to experience the normal difficulties of any human life. In-Christ people are susceptible to flat tires, bad days, taxes, and the flu. We experience times of self-doubt, confusion, and failure. We may stumble in relationships and alienate people; we may act unfairly or self-centeredly.

Observers who use human standards of righteousness to evaluate who *most* needs the grace of God may decide it's one of us. And they would be correct. We stand in constant dependence on his grace. Our hope is not in our own righteousness or self-discipline but in the power of God at work in us. God's power gives us the choice to be who we are in each decision. The more we understand who we are at the deepest level of our true self, the more we choose to be that person in daily decisions.

BENEFITS OF A BIBLICAL IDENTITY

By now you've begun to note the personal advantages of placing your identity in your relationship with God. Here are more benefits:

1. This identity will live out in the real world because it actually exists. It is not what we wish we were or long to be, but who we now are.

2. This identity carries a peaceful certainty and confidence in knowing we didn't make up the definition. God declared it.

3. This identity is stable. It remains ours when changes come in role, career, health, popularity, or usefulness.

4. This identity is positive. It allows a constructive and healthy view of ourselves.

5. This identity allows for personal growth and encourages new interests and adventures. It does nothing to box us into a narrow definition.

6. This identity is large enough for a lifetime.

7. This identity includes the Holy Spirit's steady and often surprising work in changing us. It doesn't block our perception of his work but frees us to see it.

8. This identity improves our relationships. It frees us from the need for definition by other people and frees others from the uncomfortable obligation of making us

"somebody."

9. This identity transcends all cultural ways of labeling and categorizing people, yet without denying our uniqueness and individuality.

10. This identity frees us women from limits or stereotypes. It applies equally to men and women.

WOMEN AND MEN IN CHRIST

Sometimes we women shortchange ourselves when it comes to the Scriptures. We exclude ourselves from major portions of strength which are rightfully ours. It's clear that the concepts of identity shared in this chapter were given to the entire body of Christ. *Both* male and female persons comprise that body. An in-Christ person can be of either sex. Galatians 3:28,29 puts it this way:

"There is neither Jew nor Greek, slave nor free, male nor female, for you all are one in Christ Jesus. If you belong to Christ, then you are Abraham's seed, and heirs according to the promise."

This significant statement may well have shocked the Galatian Christians. "But after all, Paul, you're a Jew and proud of it!" they may have reacted. "And like every good Jewish man, you've prayed the traditional daily prayer we're used to hearing: 'God, I thank you I was not born a woman, a slave, or a Gentile.' Have you changed your mind, Paul?"

Yes, Paul had changed his mind. His writings about various women in the ministry expressed that change, as did his relationships with women, many of whom were first-century co-ministers and co-martyrs.

This declaration's purpose does not suggest we forget we are female but shows us that our identity and power are not found in our racial heritage, political status, class, or gender.

Those identities are obsolete. Our identity and power are now found "in Christ."

When we forget this important truth, we tend to masculinize the word of God. For example, we hear people say, "the father is the priest of his home." The Bible reads this way: "To him who...has made *us* to be a kingdom and priests to serve his God and Father" (Rev. 1:5,6). (Italics mine.) Those words are meant for the entire church. Because we traditionally think of priests as male, we exclude ourselves. In truth, women in Christ are also priests unto God.

Ephesians calls us "sons of God." We miss the meaning if we speculate as to why it excludes "daughters of God." When the Bible was written, the concept of sonship implied a privileged relationship that could never be described by the use of "daughtership." The term "son of God" is a genderless concept. So, although we are female, we are also "sons of God" in that we share the inheritance and privileges of sons.

FULL HEIRS AND FULL PARTNERS

We Christian women need to live as full partners in the kingdom of God. And we need to live as full partners in the home and community, taking on adult responsibilities. The church needs both women and men of strong identity. As all members of the body of Christ share their gifts, the church is built up. The body of Christ becomes healthy, robust, functioning as it was intended to function, with *all* its parts actively working.

As we fully understand the identity God has given us, we grow in our capacity to live as women of strength. Possessing stable identity is *basic* to personal strength. No human can give us that stable identity. It is not found in a man, no matter how powerful, charming, or loving he may be. It is not found in a career, even when that career is blessed with magnificent success. Our children cannot give it to us.

Until we discover and accept our identity in Christ, we will search for it in all the wrong places, finding an illusion of identity from time to time, only to lose it with any changing wind of fortune. We will be victimized by our need to find it. We will give other persons far too much power as we let them tell us who we are (or who we are not).

Misplaced identity is a widespread problem of women in our generation. The root of countless plagues we read about in women's magazines and hear of on television stem from it: depression, low self-esteem, helplessness, battering, abuse, eating disorders, serial marriages, neglected children, relational conflicts, and yes, even abused husbands.

Who are you—really? Why not resolve it once and for all? Can you admit that God tells the truth and agree with him today? Say it out loud: "I am who God says I am. My identity is settled. I am in Christ."

FOR YOUR OWN BIBLE STUDY
Romans 8:9,17
1 Corinthians 6:19
2 Corinthians 5:17
Ephesians 1
Ephesians 2:4-6
Philippians 2:13
1 Peter 2:2
2 Peter 3:18

Chapter 4

Stable Self-Worth

Our true identity in Christ is essential to everything else that issues from our lives. Without denying our gender, race, religious heritage, or culture, identity in Christ gives definition to and understanding of who we are *first*—before we begin to see ourselves as woman or man, young or old, single or married, child or parent.

For the Christian woman or man, identity is not a goal; it's a completed fact. We don't strive to find identity through achievement, talents, or accomplishments. Our talents, work, abilities, and accomplishments only express our identity to the world around us.

DISCOVERING OUR IDENTITY

Although God establishes our new identity at the time we

become "sons of God," *we* don't automatically know who we are. We may observe that something is different, may feel like a "new creation in Christ," and quickly realize that "the old has gone, the new has come" (2 Cor. 5:17); but we discover this new creation through a process. It is not made obvious to us all at once.

Although our identity is a completed fact, our *discovery* of that identity is incomplete. It unfolds. The more we see and understand the new creation as it really is, the more easily that new creation expresses itself through our personalities. We know the process is well underway when we accept God's definition of our identity. This acknowledgement opens us to see the implications of that identity. We are more able to understand his explanation of his creative work and give up our old labels and definitions. One pleasant and long-lasting effect of this process is that our feelings of worth and value increase.

Separating the concept of identity from the concept of personal worth is difficult as they are intertwined in life. But to study them, let's take them separately.

DO WE MATTER?

We need to know who we are and *why* we matter. How much do we matter? Are we valuable? Do we have worth? After we discover our identity, our next question is, "So what?"

Again, we find good news in Scripture. We *already have* value and worth. We don't work to gain it. We are winners no matter how slow or fast we run the race. We begin by believing what God says about our value, not by trying to find a way to prove our worth. Our actions become an *expression* of our worth, rather than a means to create it.

Few subjects are more crucial to women than self-worth. Because current ways of measuring a woman's value are destructive, they have thrown many of us into fluctuating states of despair, self-doubt, and inability to live full lives. Strength is dissipated by self-doubt.

SOURCE OF WORTH

Ask yourself these challenging questions. What is the source of your self-respect? Upon what rationale do you base your worth? In other words, how, when life seems a failure, can you still hold to the idea that you matter?

Outside of a relationship with God, it's tough to answer those questions. Many people believe we are only products of biology. There is no God, no life after death. They can only guess at answers to questions like, "Why are we here? Why do we matter?"

In the book, *I'm OK, You're OK,* Thomas Harris declares that human beings must learn self-worth to be healthy. But when he questions, "Are persons important?" he can find no logical answer in the world of human knowledge. He points out that neither history nor science gives any data by which we can prove the value of individuals. And personal experience often reinforces our feelings of worthlessness.

So finally Harris says, "We cannot prove [persons] are important. We have only the faith to believe they are, because of the greater difficulty of believing they are not."[1] This is as far as we can go until we accept God's revelation of our value.

CREATED WITH VALUE

Being at sea in a universe without meaning is a frightening loneliness. But how different when we know Christ. One statement from the word of God settles forever the question of whether or not we have value as persons. "So God created man *in his own image,* in the image of God he created him; male and female he created them" (Gen. 1:27). (Italics mine.) That one fact gives us human dignity, a reason for self-respect. We are not animals. We are not an accident.

This Scripture declares that women as well as men are made in the image of God. The Hebrew words for male (*zakar*) and female (*negebah*) appear for the first time in this verse. It is not that the male half of the human race was created in the image of God and then, as a kind of afterthought, females were made to give the males someone to rule. Listen to God's intentions in creating us:

"Then God said, 'Let us make man (here the word is a generic term for humankind or humanity rather than *zakar,* the word for male), in our image, in our likeness, and *let them rule* over the fish of the sea and the birds of the air, over the livestock, over all the earth, and over all the creatures that move along the ground'" (Gen. 1:26). (Italics mine.)

From the knowledge of our creation, we gain understanding of our worth. Whether we are male or female, something about us resembles God. We carry his likeness in our human flesh.[2]

We are creatures able to have a personal relationship with God. The more we know him, the more we grow to understand our value not only as humans, but also as unique individuals.

NO SECONDS IN CREATION

This value includes the person who has special reason to doubt her usefulness because of handicaps or physical limitations. This person may learn certain skills, but her value will not increase. Handicaps, whether due to birth or accident, do not lessen the image of God nor obscure the glory of God within. Besides, we are all handicapped in some way; some handicaps are just less visible than others. If we limit ourselves by seeing only the imperfect exterior, we miss knowing valuable and gifted persons.

Some people have confided in me that they were born out of wedlock. Or that "mother had to get married." This discovery had a devastating effect on their self-worth. But to God, our beginning has *no relevance* to our value. He does not assign lesser worth to so-called "illegitimate" children. Nor does he measure value by standards like, "conceived out of wedlock," "conceived out of wedlock, but born to married parents," "conceived three days before wedlock," "born out of wedlock but adopted by a respectable family." How ridiculous to imagine God sorting through his catalog of birth dates to see where each baby would be categorized.

Others grew up knowing they were unwanted. "Daddy had hoped for a boy." Or, "Mom's birth control failed to work." Or, "I was a change-of-life baby. My parents were too old and too tired to be bothered with me." This cannot help but create self-doubt. Our earliest awareness of our worth comes from the way we are valued or not valued by our family.

This is not reality, but a misconception. Whatever the circumstances of our birth, our person is defined in the image of God. As his child, God values each of us highly.

WHY ARE WE VALUABLE?

Ask yourself these practical questions: Which of our beliefs determine our concept of self-worth? Why are we valuable? Is it because we have good looks or brains? Does our worth rest upon the amount of money we earn? Do we feel important because we have certain talents, such as a melodic voice, leadership skills, or artistic abilities? If we feel these things determine worth, chances are if we lose ground in any of these areas we also begin to lose our self-respect.

Some believe a woman finds her worth in motherhood. If so, what happens when the children are grown and no longer need her to mother them? Women often come to old age with a terrible loss of self-esteem. If our value is based on "feeling needed," then it will inevitably disintegrate at some point.

It is also a fallacy to assess a person's worth on the basis of "*no* brains, beauty, talent, skills, education, wife, husband, or people who need nurturing" to explain why he or she is *not* valuable.

SHIFTING SAND

The Scripture warns us about building our value upon a temporary foundation of "shifting sand." We are admonished to build on the lasting foundation:

"Let not the wise man boast of his wisdom or the strong man boast of his strength or the rich man boast of his riches, but *let him who boasts boast about this: that he understands and knows me,* that I am the Lord, who exercises kindness, justice and righteousness on earth" (Jer. 9:23,24). (Italics mine.)

This profound verse clearly defines the source of our self-esteem: our relationship with the Lord. We do not achieve value from accomplishments, from living in an expensive home, or being the leader of some great organization.

NINE BIBLICAL REASONS

Specifically, nine reasons for self-esteem—concrete scriptural reasons why I have value in this world—stand whether I succeed or fail. They will stand through the ups and downs of popularity or rejection. These nine statements are God's declarations of reality, not human attempts at self-assurance. For me as a believer, these remain true, whether I feel them emotionally or not.

1. **I have value because I was created in the image of God** (Gen. 1:27). Something in me is like God; that gives me infinite worth.
2. **I was a special creation from my beginning** (Ps. 139:13-16). Before my birth, God himself designed me as his individual work of art for a destiny no other human could fulfill.
3. **I am important because God considers me important** (Ps. 8:4,5; Matt. 10:29-31). He is mindful of me and cares for me. He crowned me with glory and honor. He numbers the hairs of my head and speaks of my worth to him.
4. **I am so valuable, Jesus died for me** (Rom. 5:7,8). Even as a sinner, I had value to him; I did not earn his favor by being religious or good. I have value because he loves me.
5. **Christ lives in me** (2 Cor. 4:7; Gal. 2:20). I have access to all the knowledge and wisdom of God because Christ lives in me. I am a repository of true wealth.
6. **I am now God's work of art** (Eph. 2:10). I am a masterpiece in the making. I am his workmanship. He's continuing the artwork he started nine months before my birth. "What we will be has not yet been made known" (1 John 3:2), but he is forming something unique and wondrous in me.
7. **God accepts me as I am right now** (Eph. 1:4). As a new creation, he pronounces me holy and blameless—

good. (Sound familiar—like a replay of another time? God looked at his creation and "it was very good" (Gen. 1:31).

8. **I am a source of pleasure to God** (Ps. 147:11; 149:4; Zeph. 3:17). He enjoys me. As I find pleasure in my children, God finds delight in his people.

9. **God is working in me and will continue to do so as long as I live** (Phil. 1:6). "Being confident of this, that he who began a good work in you will carry it on to completion until the day of Christ Jesus." That means I have value at any age even if not one person in the world needs me or desires my company. He will continue the good work he has begun, and I will be the focus of his interest and attention.

These are only a sampling of the reasons for our value listed in Scripture. We discover them all through the Bible—as though God were trying in every way possible to tell us over and over, *"You're important.* You're important to me. You're valuable beyond measure."

WE'RE SUPPOSED TO BE HUMBLE

Doesn't the Bible tell us to be humble? It does. Christian humility is not maintaining a low view of ourselves. No virtue is found in having an inferiority complex or in declaring our worthlessness. We are not inferior because we haven't achieved a popular athletic status, won a beauty contest, gone to college, held a job, or been a preacher or missionary. God doesn't count the number of talents we've developed or the amount of money we've accumulated and then decide where we rate on his scale of superior, mediocre, or inferior. We are precious to God just as our children are precious to us, infinitely valuable, loved just because they're our children.

So then, what does God want if he asks us to be humble?

THE IDEAL CHRISTIAN WOMAN

I once thought Christian humility was to apologize for what I was not and to remind people of what I ought to be. I'd heard sermons telling me what I should be...sermons effective in shaming me and bringing me to confessions of guilt. I thought it was spiritual to feel condemned when I did not measure up. The churchly standard for the Christian woman is, we must admit, hardly attained by anyone we know. Still, it is spoken of as though it were the norm.

Although this standard is vaguely defined, we have had the general idea that the Christian woman is always sweet, saintly, peaceful, patient, and kind. She raises angelic children, keeps an orderly household, takes in the needy, and ministers day and night. She never shows tiredness, anger, confusion, or fear. She is a pristine beauty, having no ugly brown age spots, no wet places under the arms, no panty lines. Her hair always stays in place. She is in perfect aerobic condition, eats only healthy foods, and exercises daily (only to Christian music, of course). No cellulite or horrid fat cells are found on her body. No extra hairs in incorrect places, no zits, dry skin, oily skin, wrinkles, or laugh lines mar her perfection.

The Christian woman attends diet classes, Bible studies, and prayer meetings. She wears the latest fashions and keeps her nails nicely polished. Besides all this, she is successful in a career and known as a community leader.

No wonder we sit in church services and become discouraged trying to envision Christianity lived out by a woman of our day. Our image of *the Christian woman* allows for little humanness. We become disheartened as we see the unbridgable gap between ourselves and her perfection, especially when voices everywhere remind us.

We can't win. As we compare ourselves, buzzards in the world of peacocks, we begin to feel inferior. Feeling inferior has one small gratification. Aha! "I think I have at least *one* saintly quality—humility."

But the truth is, we haven't even that.

BIBLICAL HUMILITY

True humility is having an *accurate* view of ourselves. We see ourselves not as more or less valuable than others but as vital parts of the body of Christ.

> For by the grace given me I say to every one of you: Do not think of yourself more highly than you ought, but rather think of yourself with sober [accurate] judgment, in accordance with the measure of faith God has given you. Just as each of us has one body with many members, and these members do not all have the same function, so in Christ we who are many form one body, and each member belongs to all the others (Rom. 12:3-5).

Each part of the body of Christ is valuable. What each of us gives is needed. No one is superior or inferior. With relief, we can abandon the image of the perfect Christian woman.

When this becomes our attitude, we'll neither have an inferiority complex nor be conceited. We'll not only like ourselves but also like others without attempting to change them into our image.

There's often a thin line between self-worth and conceit, between self-acceptance and smug satisfaction. For instance, if I've accepted myself just as I am, with all known weaknesses and virtues, does that mean I think I've arrived? Am I saying to the world, "Look everybody! Here I am...the perfect woman. Imitate me and you can be perfect too!" No! That is a perversion of self-worth. We instinctively reject that attitude, because we know it denies the value of our individual differences and maturing processes.

WORTH IS NOT PERFECTION

True self-worth is not blind. "We have this treasure in jars of clay" (2 Cor. 4:7). We are so valuable we contain the very glory of God himself, but so human that the container is compared to a cheap clay pot. We must never forget that paradoxical truth about ourselves. We can't deny or gloss over our weaknesses, failures, or immaturities. We recognize our utter dependence on God to fill this earthen vessel with his righteousness and his person. Thus we can be honest with ourselves, call sin sin, failure failure, pride pride. Self-deception is not needed to convince us of any imagined perfection.

In a biblical understanding of self-worth, we can view ourselves as important to God, to the body of Christ, and to an effective ministry to the world. At the same time, we in no way deny that others are just as valuable, even those who may be different than we are. In fact, true self-worth recognizes that we need people who are completely different from us. Only then can we be at peace with ourselves, with other men and women. Released to love without restraint, we can admire and enjoy one another.

The implications of this biblical attitude are far-reaching when it comes to relationships. Rather than assess a person's relative worth by looks, sex appeal, money, or popularity, we are free to see the real person. True understanding becomes a possibility when we drop the evaluation games and begin a relationship having decided the other person is valuable.

This basis for worth transcends (and yet includes) an individual's femaleness or maleness. Whatever Scripture tells us about the value of men is equally true for women. As women, our worth is not measured by the men in our lives (or lack of them). Our value has nothing to do with marital status, desirability to men, or assessed talents for motherhood. Our value is separate from our ability to adapt to male needs or our successes or failures in marriage, parenting, or career. This is good news for women who have difficulty relating to men because they feel intimidated by them.

WE CAN'T INCREASE OUR VALUE

We must not mistakenly assume such inspiring women as Deborah, Abigail, Priscilla, or Mary *gained* value by their accomplishments. We will not become more precious to God, more loved by him, or more valuable to him if we follow their examples. Abraham and David were accepted by God and greatly loved in the face of obvious failures. The lives of Sarah, Rahab, and Bathsheba show this same grace toward women.

Those of us in public leadership must recognize this truth. For example, if I were to lead my Bible study group in a discussion of passages about women such as Proverbs 31, Titus 2:3-5, or 1 Peter 3:1-6, I must be careful not to teach in such a way that implies these verses are a description of how to *become* a worthy woman. I must not entitle my message "How To Become Valuable To God" or "How To Win God's Favor."

We can't imply these passages are meant to define "the woman's role" or to say that their instructions for relationships apply *only* to women, as though those instructions were not also given specifically to men in other biblical passages. As leaders, it is important that we not inadvertently use the Bible to reinforce feelings of worthlessness already present in women. We must rather emphasize to women that those feelings are *not* grounded in God's opinion of them.

STRENGTH IN OUR VALUE

We have been dealing with common problems of self-doubt. As we discover solid reasons for our value apart from circumstances, we can hold our heads high and stand tall.

We are important. God believes we possess infinite value. We *are* women of worth, period.

Along with our biblical identity, this inner knowledge of our worth is an essential part of our strength. If we know our worth we are not easily intimidated. We do not allow ourselves to be mistreated, victimized, or abused. We stand up for ourselves and refuse coercion or manipulation. We resist those things which devalue women, including self-abuse, self-punishment, and destructive personal habits. We treat ourselves as God treats us, believing his assessment of our value.

Ordinary Women—Extraordinary Strength

FOR YOUR OWN BIBLE STUDY
Genesis 1:26-31
Psalm 139:13-18
Romans 5:7,8
Colossians 2:2,3
1 John 3:2

Chapter 5

Strong at
the Center

When I realized how much the Bible talks about our relationship with God as the central issue—that we are "in Christ and Christ in us," it caused me to question the way we talk and live. We tend to compartmentalize life into the sacred and the secular, the religious and the nonreligious. For example, we speak about people devoting themselves to "full-time service to God." Christians often say, "Get your priorities right." And we sing, "Jesus, others, and you..."

As a young adult, I questioned these ideas and eventually concluded that Jesus was involved in *everything* I was doing, whether school, study, work, or church activities. The closeness of my friendship with God made it impossible to separate my life into categories. At youth meetings where we were challenged to dedicate ourselves to "full-time service," I wondered how a Christian could be part time. Was I serving God only at times when I was praying or working "in the church"? Isn't service to Christ full time—twenty-four hours a day—no matter what the occupation?

GOD'S WILL FOR OUR LIVES

Nevertheless, I listened earnestly to the appeals commonly given in these meetings. I learned it was important to "find God's will for my life" in order to be a *strong* Christian. Sometimes it seemed I was being taught a Christian "formula" for success. Doing God's will meant choosing the right college and career and marrying the right person. My intense concern for *doing* the correct Christian thing may have been related to a fear of making decisions. Like many young adults, I hoped to find the correct plan and thus make God responsible for my "success." Of course, if I failed, it proved I obviously didn't choose the correct path...I missed God's will. Few could escape the ensuing guilt. Along with the guilt came loss of strength—because strength is tied to our feelings of success.

A more mature understanding of what it means to "do God's will" acknowledges the "becoming" process in our spiritual growth. We learn to follow God's guidance, know his voice, and work with his purposes. God's will is not a life plan we determine once and for all nor a set of correct decisions. Its dimensions grow as we grow in him. As God lives his life through our personalities, the *doing* is an outgrowth of our character. The new nature inside expresses itself. Our outward actions spring from inward growth rather than from past conditioning. It's a very different strength from that tied to success and failure.

This viewpoint affects "priorities." Having right priorities is usually discussed along with finding God's will for our lives. It is misleading and impractical to put God as a priority at the top of a list. He is *not* priority—he is *central*. As the center of my life, he is present in *all* my thoughts whether they focus on "religious" subjects or practical: money, work, play, or children.

God is interested in *all* of a woman's daily concerns. He participates in what may seem trivial to some: potty training, fussy babies, leaky faucets, and income taxes. Because Jesus is in us, we bring to all these activities—our careers, education, parenting, or relationships—his suggestions, his thoughts, his opinions. He is working in us "both *to will* and to act according to his good purpose" (Phil. 2:13). (Italics mine.)

GOD IS NOT A PRIORITY

Aware of our dependency on him, we receive his life as our life wherever we are, whatever we're doing. Our relationship "in Christ" is the basis of our identity. If we believe that, then we cannot relate to God as our top priority. To be strong, we must be dependent upon God, the Source of our life.

When we hear a Christian admonition to "get our priorities right," we tend to confuse this with the kind of priorities we need in time management, office management, or organizing a household. We have an imaginary picture of God's priorities for us. Let's say, for example, the list includes ten items:

1. God
2. Husband
3. Children
4. Church
5. Job
6. Friends

73

7. Homemaking   9. Ministry

8. Extended family   10. Hobbies/personal needs

In trying to divide our time according to each priority's position on the list, we meet the problem, "If God is number one, then why are my children, husband, and home taking the largest amount of time?"

Many of us believed that this list of priorities was our assignment, our responsibility, what God expected of us. If idolatry can be defined as getting our priorities out of line, we'd be idolators continuously! Living by a list of priorities simply doesn't work. Every day would be Gloom's Day— inevitable failure.

JESUS IN CONTROL

Picture a mobile. (See Figure 1) The piece in the center that holds it together is "Jesus Christ." Attached to that center, but constantly moving in relationship to one another, would be items like work, ministry, friends, home, career, church, marriage, children, housework, money...the items which make up our lives. Jesus holds them all together, gives them meaning and coordination. He's in control of all the moving parts of the mobile. If we were asked what we were doing at any given point in a day, we could answer, "I'm living for Jesus. I'm also living with Jesus."

Maybe the item uppermost on the mobile today is grocery shopping. Tomorrow it may focus on the needs of one child. At other times, our careers may require full attention. Or we may be relaxing with our husbands. We no longer need worry about monitoring the order we give each item. Christ is controlling the parts of our lives. This verse makes it clear: "And he died for all, that those who live should *no longer live for themselves but for him who died for them* and was raised again" (2 Cor. 5:15). (Italics mine.)

Once Christ is established as central, he may lead us to prioritize at times in order to accomplish his specific purposes. But this can't be set in concrete or become a new list of laws. Jesus can rearrange these areas of our lives and decide which needs attention.

Figure 1

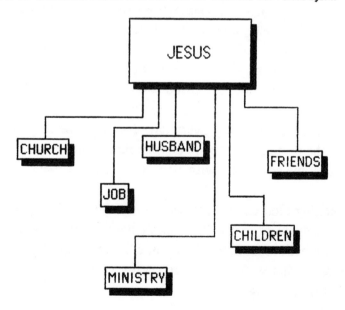

2 Corinthians 5:15 "And he died for all, that those who live should no longer live for themselves but for him who died for them and was raised again."

ALL THESE THINGS ADDED

Some have used the verse, "Seek first his kingdom and his righteousness, and all these things will be given you as well" (Matt. 6:33), as a text on priorities. Instead, this verse is about values, about our focus and perspective, about our relationship with God. When *that* becomes the central issue, daily concerns fall into place. Our eternal values give proper meaning to the daily duties related to shelter, food, and clothing.

Another way of illustrating this relationship is to draw two circles. (See Figure 2) In the center circle, write "God." Around that circle, draw a second circle in which we write our name, (The Believer). In the large circle marked The Believer, list the elements of your personality: interests, needs, goals, creativity, emotions. Arrows from the second circle point to the world, home, church, family, society, friends— the various things we relate to. In those relationships, we are Jesus' instrument—he lives through us. He is the ultimate reason for, the motive and the source of, both our desires and our actions. We live in communion with him, a fellowship which continues all day every day. The more we respond to him, the more aware we are of what he's doing in the world. We become coworkers with him. His strength flows through us.

Making God central affects our vocabulary. How do we replace the word priority? Saying we have no priorities sounds like we believe nothing really matters...as though it were irrelevant what we do with our energy or time.

(Figure 2 on page 77)

WHAT'S IMPORTANT?

Saying God is not a priority may seem equivalent to saying he's not important or that he matters like grass or

Figure 2

Galatians 2:20 "I have been crucified with Christ and I no longer live, but Christ lives in me. The life I live in the body, I live by faith in the Son of God, who loved me and gave himself for me."

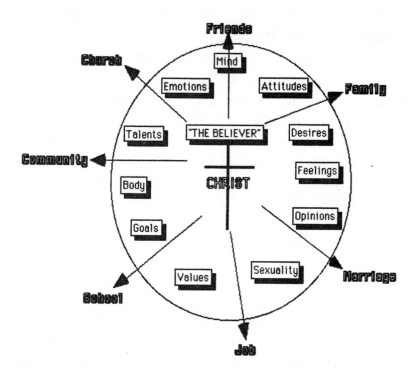

For a complete Scripture description of the above concept, see John 15:19

silverware or television. Is that the direction we're headed if we do not have a list of priorities? Are we left floundering without direction, hoping to find meaning in whatever we happen to experience? Does personal holiness disappear since we have decided it's not a priority to pray or study the Scriptures or "work for God"? These are important questions.

PRIORITIES IN THE EARLY CHURCH

Consider the early Christians. They didn't live meaningless lives but were strong people who lived with a vital sense of purpose, goal, and direction. They were so convinced of God's will for their lives that they died for their convictions. But they did not die because Jesus was a priority. They lived and died because he was all in all!

The apostle Paul was so sure of God's will for his life that he declared, "Woe to me if I do not preach the gospel!" (1 Cor. 9:16). He understood the tie between personal fulfillment and God's call. In order to carry out God's calling, Paul was willing to travel difficult journeys, suffer pain and hunger, work at hard manual labor to support himself, forego the comforts of home, and suffer persecution.

It appears Paul placed a high priority on preaching the gospel. But in fact, the way he expressed it was, "for to me, to *live* is Christ" (Phil. 1:21); "so that now as always Christ will be exalted in my body, whether by life or by death" (Phil. 1:20). He also said, "I consider everything a loss compared to the surpassing greatness of knowing Christ Jesus my Lord" (Phil. 3:8).

These are his statements about the will of God and his relationship to God. He didn't see God as number one on a list. He saw his relationship to God as motivating and directing every decision of his life. No wonder this man seemed so invincible.

Values might better describe a Christian's way of living. What is the difference between making choices based on our values rather than on a list of priorities?

A priority applies to doing, to the order in which work is done, people are contacted, or needs met. Priorities are necessary in running an office or managing time. We decide which things to do first, second, third; which letters need to go out today or which calls are most urgent.

Values apply to the *reasons* for doing. Priorities may change from week to week or even from day to day. But our values provide the ongoing reasons for our doing these things. A woman of strength is one who is growing in her values.

GROWTH IN OUR VALUES

At our Wednesday Bible study, I asked, "How are your values changing as you grow in Christ? Or, to put it another way, can you identify any changes in the things you value since you have become a Christian?" As women shared their answers, we noticed some common experiences.

A shift in values toward people and relationships was reflected in statements like, "I've become more tolerant of others—more accepting and less demanding of them." Some said they valued people more; things less. Many said this shift led to a lifestyle they hadn't anticipated. No one instructed them, "Now that you are a Christian, you must get your priorities right. Build your lifestyle on a new set of priorities." No, the Holy Spirit changes our values. It is a continuous work. I've been a Christian since childhood, and it is still going on.

In recent years, I find I value achievement less and people more. Success, at least in terms of our society's definition, is less important than relationships, family, the body of Christ, freedom, and integrity. The Spirit's adjustment of our values also affects the way we see ourselves as individuals.

For example, I now value parts of my life that in earlier years seemed unimportant. Emotions for one. I haven't always understood that God considers our emotions valuable, not just feelings to be pushed aside in favor of cold rationality. He doesn't regard them as part of a "lower nature" or "old man" but as a vital part of the redeemed person I now am. In fact, my mind and emotions are not intended to work in conflict as a dichotomy, but in harmony, as one.

I've come to value authenticity—the ability to be a *real* person complete with failures, foibles, successes, tears, tiredness—all that humanness includes. I've also come to value the unique qualities God placed in me; my spontaneity, "socialness," musical tastes, and skills. I value my enthusiasm for life, a curious mind, and natural love for study.

I value the guidance of the Holy Spirit, which is not mere reasoning, not simply calculating a decision and acting on it logically (although I may *appear* to live that way since I don't often say, "the Lord told me..."). I make choices and decisions out of my values, which he is transforming. This is part of his way of guiding.

But even more than that, I'm aware of God's immediate presence. Jesus promised we would experience the Comforter (see John 14 and 15), the Guide who would walk beside us and teach us how to work with God in the reconciliation of men to him. At times he may urge me to do something beyond my understanding—a choice I would not think to make if I looked *only* to my set of facts and values.

When we live out of our values rather than from a list of

priorities, we must still have the guidance of the Holy Spirit. Even a clear-cut, well-defined set of values will never be the sole source of direction because our values are yet incomplete. God has information at his disposal that we do not have. God must always be the Sovereign Lord, heard and obeyed by his servants. The confidence in knowing we have guidance outside ourselves is another part of a Christian woman's strength.

THE VALUE OF WORSHIP

In this same context, worship becomes a major value. We don't go to church to prove we're pious. We don't do it to get God to like us. It's not to manipulate God into answering our prayers. We're busy people. Why on earth would we spend precious hours every week in church services? Our emotions are often uncooperative. We may feel tired, grouchy, withdrawn, or sad. But our choices are not made from emotions. They're made from our values.

If God is central in our lives, if relationship with him is the controlling reality, then worship becomes important. It reinforces and strengthens our commitment to him. It is how we express our love to him.

RESPONDING TO GOD

God continuously loves us unconditionally; he gives to us and serves us. But relationship does not develop when one person does all the serving and the other passively receives. Mutual giving and receiving are necessary to develop a relationship.

Worship is the primary way in which we can respond to God. Christians of every era have spent large amounts of time worshiping together. They've delighted in it; they've taken it seriously. Maybe at times they've taken it too seriously. But worship has been the essence of their times together and the basis for their fellowship. Given our relationship with God, this is natural.

TRUE WORSHIP

When lovemaking has to be put on a calendar and a wife has to demand her monthly session, chances are something is wrong in that relationship. When affection has to be regimented in a relationship, one person is choosing not to respond, whether for reasons of self-consciousness, guilt, inhibition, fear, or selfishness.

In the same way, when worship is legislated or made a legalistic requirement for holiness, something has gone wrong with our values.

Worship may be enjoyed alone, with a small group, or with a large group. However and whenever we worship, it always takes place because we value our relationship with our Father. For me the habit of worship will continue, not as a priority, but from a desire to know God. Some worship takes place in the midst of my work day but far too little to satisfy my needs. So I'm a habitual churchgoer, even if church attendance doesn't appear on my list of priorities.

LIVING OUT OF OUR VALUES

The same concept is true of "Christian duties" such as prayer, Bible reading, or evangelism. As we continue in the process of becoming who we are in Christ, our living becomes a consistent, creative expression of his values to the world around us. We don't live religiously, following lists of spiritual duties to prove ourselves saved. We read the Bible and pray because we love God and desire to understand him.

Witnessing is a natural result of that love coupled with the awareness that others need to experience relationship with God also. It arises from the knowledge that we have good news to share.

This practical, sensible way of living a natural Christian life opens the door to freedom from lists which were formerly called "roles." A woman's "role" and a man's "role" were comprised of different lists of priorities. In many homes, playing the roles correctly became a substitute for real Christianity.

We do not need a relationship with God to play a role. But to live out of our values and out of true spiritual guidance— that *does* necessitate a relationship with God. A strong woman is not play-acting. She is genuine.

Ordinary Women—Extraordinary Strength
FOR YOUR OWN BIBLE STUDY
Scriptures to Study
2 Corinthians 5:15
Galatians 2:20
Philippians 3:8,9

Chapter 6

When Strong Women Fall in Love

How does our new-found strength affect our marriages? Do we jeopardize our relationship with our husbands by using the strength God gives? Will we overpower our mates and end up alone and lonely?

No. Rather we have a far better chance at success in marriage than the woman who feigns weakness and dependency. Because the basis of our relationship with our husbands is mutual respect, we can sustain romantic love over the years and through difficult times.

Aristotle observed, "Friendship ideally consists of a relationship between equals."[1]

He may have been the first, but not the last, writer to point out that friendship is a relationship between equals. In the twelfth century, a Cistercian monk, Aelred of Rivelaux, wrote *On Spiritual Friendship*. Not many celibate monks held a positive attitude toward women, but Aelred was an exception. He wrote:

When God created man...It was from no similar, nor even from the same material that divine Might formed this help mate, but as a clearer inspiration to charity and friendship he produced the woman from the very substance of man. How beautiful it is that the second human being was taken from the side of the first, *so that nature might teach that human beings are equal and as it were, collateral, and that there is in human affairs neither a superior nor an inferior, a characteristic of true friendship.*[2] (Italics mine.)

If equality is basic to friendship, then it is even more necessary to enduring romantic love—not the kind a teenager feels for a first fling and then again only weeks later for the current singing star or movie idol—but that love which lasts.

Both infatuation and romantic love *can occur* between unequals. But genuine romantic love can only last when equality is felt by both people in the relationship.

ROMANCE IS NOT MAGIC

Nathaniel Branden, recognized authority on romantic love after thirty years as a psychotherapist, demonstrated it is not a mysterious, magical, uncontrollable phenomenon. He observed:

We have long been witness to the fact that many persons begin a relationship genuinely in love and with goodwill and high hopes for the future, and then across time, tragically, painfully, and with a good deal of bewilderment, watch the relationship deteriorate and ultimately collapse. They think back to a time when they were deeply in love, when so much seemed right and good and rewarding, and they are tortured by not knowing how and why they lost what they had. If *that* love could die, they find themselves feeling can *any* love last? Is romantic love possible for me at all? Or for anyone? Perhaps it's time to put the dream away along with the rest of the toys of childhood. And sometimes they reach a day when even these questions are forgotten, when the anguish of why and how has long since faded, and all that is left is numbness.[3]

WHAT IS ROMANTIC LOVE?

Branden defines romantic love:

Romantic love is a passionate spiritual-emotional-sexual attachment between a man and a woman that reflects a high regard for the value of each other's person. I do not describe the relationship as romantic love if there is not some experience of spiritual affinity, some deep mutuality of values and outlook, some sense of being "soul mates"; if there is not deep emotional involvement; if there is not a strong sexual attraction. And if there is not mutual admiration—if, for example, there is mutual contempt instead—again I do not describe the relationship as romantic love.[4]

In Branden's work and also the works of many Christian therapists, we see repeated conclusions about the importance of *mutual* respect, clear communication with freedom to share feelings and thoughts without censure.

No amount of counseling can restore romantic love to a marriage in which one person is viewed as inferior or less respected or admired than the other.

IMMATURE LOVE

The destruction or loss of romance is tied to immature love, the kind of love which motivates one person to either an unhealthy dependency or an unhealthy domination.

For example: using military systems as a model for family life puts the husband in the position of commander in chief over the wife. This pattern may bring a certain predictability, but it will guarantee the downfall of romance.

If a woman is told that God ordained her to take a lesser role, to carry less responsibility, to be less able to think clearly and make decisions, to only follow and never to lead, she will, in accepting this self-image, eventually be able to love only in a dependent fashion, more as a child than as an adult. She cannot accept her God-given strength or believe in her value. She is unable to experience a genuine, enduring romantic love relationship.

Immature love cannot last. Unequal love cannot last. The woman who chooses to be helpless and dependent fails to grasp the truth of the greater joy that could be hers as a woman of strength and equality.

ROMANCE LOST

Jerry and I are in Copenhagen. In this romantic setting, we can look across the water and see Sweden. We came to Denmark to speak at conferences. It's springtime, and the trees have budded. Flowers are in full bloom, and the birds sing day and night. It's a beautiful place, and we feel romantic as we walk hand in hand along the shore. We love each other, and it feels good.

But I remember many such trips where our feelings were less than romantic. Those memories call forth feelings of strange alienation, of emotional distance, of loneliness in our togetherness. As in this trip, we ministered together in conferences, met new friends, experienced the challenge of new cultures, and taught through an interpreter. But we did not feel "in love." If I gave it any serious thought during those times, I found myself weeping. What had happened to the romance we once enjoyed? Why had we fallen out of love?

WHEN FEELINGS ARE GONE

Many couples experience this. I knew that. And I knew they generally say, "I'm just not in love anymore" and walk away. There appear to be only two alternatives: 1) to get a divorce or 2) to grit your teeth and hang in there by the grace of God to live out the rest of your life in a marriage that has no emotions, affection, or warmth. Both alternatives absolutely terrified me.

For a time we tried to ignore our problems. Then came a few years of painful struggle when we vacillated between giving up and trying harder. We thought we knew a lot about marriage. But much of what I had read in Christian books assumed a structure which called for dictatorship by the husband and absolute subjection by the wife. Many women believed their marriage problems would be solved if they simply "submitted" more and quit "rebelling."

SPLIT PERSONALITY

Equality was present in the relationship we began in college. Two strong personalities admired and respected one another, happily joined their goals and dreams to build a life. We felt no power struggle in our early marriage and no concern with questions about "final authority."

We had used the Taylor Johnson Temperament Analysis test for pre-marital counseling at the church. Thinking it might be helpful in discovering our own problems, I decided to take it myself and asked Jerry to join me in reviewing the results.

I took the test twice—once as Barbara Cook and a second time as Mrs. Jerry Cook. My answers to the test questions were dependent on whether I was playing the role of Jerry's wife or acting as myself.

The two tests revealed two drastically different people. Barbara appeared on the graph as confident, outgoing, expressive, cheerful, and optimistic. Mrs. Jerry Cook was passive, nonexpressive, submissive; and in many parts of the graph, her personality was in the area marked "improvement urgent."

In an effort to be a good Christian wife, to prove my loyalty and spirituality, I had submitted myself right out of existence!

In public life or with friends, I was a confident person, usually outgoing and talkative. But at home, I behaved as a dutiful, quiet wife, giving my husband what I believed he wanted, what I'd been taught his male ego was created to need: compliance, agreement, obedience to the slightest suggestion.

"I hate this wife-woman!" Jerry said as he saw the tests. "This one is the girl I love," he said, pointing to the "Barbara" test.

Those words were revelational to me. Could it be he was not like men were said to be? Were his needs different from what I had been led to believe?

Basic questions about the nature of men and women became part of my study. Were men really created to rule women? Was there a correlation between the loneliness in our marriage and the *system* we had built for the relationship? Our system, or structure, provided definitions of roles, told us who was to perform what functions. Could we live as a family without such a structure?

We had been told that the only alternatives to "God's order for the family" were anarchy or unbridled female dominance. No mention was made of alternatives such as cooperation, joint decision-making, and mutual respect.

I looked for answers in the Bible.

CLUES IN THE BIBLE

The Scriptures have at least one clear statement on the subject. Whatever our system, as Christians we are not allowed to control or dominate one another:

> You know that those who are regarded as rulers of the Gentiles *lord it over them,* and their high officials *exercise authority over them.* Not so with you. Instead, whoever wants to become great among you must be your servant, and whoever wants to be first must be slave of all (Mark 10:42-45). (Italics mine.)

Philippians 2:1-8 presents a way in which strong persons are to relate in Christ:

> If you have any encouragement from being united with Christ, if any comfort from his love, if any fellowship with the Spirit, if any tenderness and compassion, then make my joy complete by being like-minded, having the same love, being one in spirit and purpose. Do nothing out of selfish ambition or vain conceit, but in humility consider others better than yourselves. Each of you should look not only to your own interests, but also to the interests of others.
>
> Your attitude should be the same as that of Christ Jesus: Who, being in very nature God, did not con-

sider equality with God something to be grasped, but made himself nothing, taking the very nature of a servant, being made in human likeness.

And being found in appearance as a man, he humbled himself and became obedient to death—even death on a cross!

This description leaves no room for controlling, commanding, or ruling over another person.

RESURRECTION OF A RELATIONSHIP

So where did Jerry and I go wrong?

We systematically destroyed romantic love as we lived out our erroneous beliefs about men and women. The romance of two rational Christian people degenerated. We should have known better, should have more intelligently structured our marriage.

In his book *The Romance Factor,* Christian psychologist Alan Loy McGinnis, writes about "dwindling into a wife":

"Not only must one enter a love relationship with a good identity formation; it is also essential to maintain one's individuality. This has been easier for men than for women, given our society's expectation that a woman is built to be dependent. Although she may have been functioning as an independent, self-starting person before the marriage—while in college, for instance—she is, in William Congreve's phrase, often expected to "dwindle" into a wife.

For all the traditionalists' talk about the glories of being a homemaker, wife and mother (and there are indeed many aspects of glory in these roles), we see all too many women lose ground in personal development and self-esteem during the early and middle years of adulthood, whereas men are gaining ground during the same years as they compete and achieve in the working world. We see women who are quite able to take care of themselves before marriage but who become helpless after fifteen or twenty years of marriage. Psychiatrist Genevieve Knupfer describes a woman who had managed several foreign tours before marriage; when widowed at the age of fifty-five, she had to ask friends how to get a passport."[5]

DIVORCE

Jerry and I did something smart. We have never regretted it. Rather than divorce one another, we divorced our old marriage. Piece by piece, we tore apart the structure we had mindlessly built over the years. We carefully scrutinized all our beliefs about marriage, men, women, strength, and authority.

The death process of the old marriage was painful. But the joy of a resurrected relationship replaced the pain. With amazement and gratitude we have watched romance return.

KNIGHTS AND LADIES

One of the hardest assumptions for me to give up was the notion that romantic love thrives only in an environment of male dominance. I connected romance with the knight in shining armor rescuing the helpless princess from evil dragons. In keeping with the myths of medieval chivalry, I liked the pedestal woman and the strong, courageous he-man. I could not conceive of romance between two equals, where both alternately rescue and protect each other.

I believed that men felt romantic about fascinating women and total women, and that these must fit into the Bible somewhere. Without my awareness, this misbelief led me to camouflage my strength, pretend to be less intelligent than I was (in the presence of men), and even try to feel more squeamish about spiders and snakes. How can a gallant knight feel tenderness toward a woman who kills her own spiders?

Romance was high on my list of desirables; and with genuine grief, I gave up as untrue and unbiblical the notions that to me were associated with it. I thought I was giving up romance.

But my notions were wrong—dead wrong. Romance may *happen* to an inferior and superior, but it will not last. The feelings of intimacy, joy, affection, and passion which characterize enduring romantic love are feelings generated in a relationship of equals. Both admire and respect one another. Neither feels manipulated, controlled, or used.

SILENT RESENTMENT

Romance thrives on the expression of emotions, not the repression of them in deference to "male authority." The years of hiding my feelings from Jerry were a total waste of energy.

I can remember thinking of myself as a godly, submitted wife on days I silently resented Jerry's "bad moods." Quoting 1 Peter 3:1, I congratulated myself and thought how well controlled I was to remain gracious. Actually I was building up a stone wall of resentment and anger that would inevitably block feelings of love. This kind of "holiness" is nothing to be proud of.

Jerry no longer has to be the knight in shining armor, my all-powerful protector, lord, and king. He is a human being who, like myself, sometimes gives protection and sometimes receives it.

We were more than glad to abandon our image of me as

the princess, pedestaled above the cares of the world, looking down upon the work and suffering of the earth. I became a woman who actively participates as God always intended. After all, in the beginning he made woman and man ruling and having dominion together.

I am not always docile, innocent, or sheltered from reality. I don't need that. I need, rather, to live a full-orbed life. And I have the strength to live that way; I am enabled by a supernatural life source, the Holy Spirit within.

Ordinary Women—Extraordinary Strength

FOR YOUR OWN BIBLE STUDY

Relationships of Mutual Respect:

   Mark 10:42-45

   Philippians 2:1-8

Romantic Love:

   Song of Songs (entire book)

   Hosea 2

   1 Corinthians 13

Chapter 7

Women of Might and Power

When I discovered that the virtuous woman of Proverbs 31 was actually the mighty woman, the powerful woman, or even the valiant woman, I became excited. I felt like a sea explorer who had just discovered a new continent. Like Christopher Columbus, I rushed ashore to plant my flag in the newfound soil. He claimed the new world for Queen Isabella and King Ferdinand. I was slightly more selfish. "I claim this for Barbara!" I said to myself. "This *chayil* woman captures my respect. She is whom I desire to be."

Several months later, I made another exciting discovery. I remember the moment of insight, the exhilarating "aha!" moment. The *chayil* idea was clearly and deliberately continued from the Old Testament right into the New.

JEWISH PEOPLE AND A GREEK BIBLE

In Jesus' day, the Jews didn't use a Hebrew Bible. A few hundred years before Christ was born, Greek became the everyday, common language used for commerce and business and politics. Like everyone else, the Jews learned Greek. The Old Testament was written in Hebrew so the Jews had seventy of their best wise men translate the Old Testament into Greek.

The translators found a Greek word which matched *chayil.* They used that Greek word in nearly all the places where *chayil* appeared. If we were to read the *chayil* verses (listed in chapter 1) in the Septuagint (the name they gave the new Greek translation), we would see this word instead of *chayil.*

THE SECOND AHA!

The word: *DUNAMIS.* The same word from which we get dynamite. Or dynamic.

Our valiant Proverbs example is a dynamite woman. She's not only strong, mighty, powerful, and valiant, she's also dynamic!

When Jesus went to church, he read from the Septuagint which talked about *dunamis.* He knew the *dunamis* woman of Proverbs 31 and about David's *dunamis* men of war and all the *dunamis* heroes of old.

When the Holy Spirit directed the writers of the New Testament to use *dunamis,* it packed a rich meaning for the first readers of the New Testament.

Jesus used *dunamis* to explain what would happen when the Holy Spirit came upon his followers:

"But you will receive *power (dunamis)* when the Holy Spirit comes on you; and you will be my witnesses in Jerusalem, and in all Judea and Samaria, and to the ends of the earth" (Acts 1:8).

We see it again in Colossians 1:11:

"Being strengthened with all *power* according to his glorious might so that you may have great endurance and patience."

And again in Romans 15:19:

"By the *power* of signs and miracles, through the *power* of the Spirit." (Italics mine.)

So, *dunamis in the New Testament was used in the same way as chayil in the Old Testament.* Translated power, might, or authority, it referred to a *certain kind* of power. Before we can understand this power, we need to look at another word often used for power.

EXOUSIA: DELEGATED AUTHORITY

Out of the available words for power, authority, and might, Jesus chose two to speak of the power of his followers. One was *dunamis;* the other, *exousia. Exousia* refers to *delegated* authority. If we have *exousia,* we have been given the right to act on another's behalf. In the United States, we call it power of attorney.

When my husband and I travel overseas, we give certain people power of attorney to use in our absence. It consists of a document stating that Mr. So-and-so has been given the right to sign business papers and make decisions in our name. If an emergency arises in our absence, he has the power (legal ability) to act on our behalf.

POWER OF ATTORNEY

Power of attorney was useful when we adopted Sundar. We mailed legal documents overseas to give power of attorney (*exousia*) to a woman who would represent us in an Indian court. This lady acted in our stead, as though she were Mr. and Mrs. Cook standing before the judge petitioning to adopt

Sundar.

Jesus spoke often about giving *exousia,* or legal authority, to his followers:

"When Jesus had called the Twelve together, he gave them power and authority (*exousia*) to drive out all demons and to cure diseases" (Luke 9:1).

"I have given you authority (*exousia*) to trample on snakes and scorpions and to overcome all the power (*dunamis*) of the enemy; nothing will harm you" (Luke 10:19).

"Yet to all who received him, to those who believed in his name, he gave the right (*exousia*) to become children of God" (John 1:12).

Jesus explained to his disciples about the changes that would come after he went away:

"In that day you will no longer ask me anything. I tell you the truth, my Father will give you whatever you ask *in my name.* Until now you have not asked for anything in my name. Ask and you will receive, and your joy will be complete" (John 16:23,24).

"I am telling you now before it happens, so that when it does happen you will believe that I am He. I tell you the truth, whoever accepts anyone I send accepts me; and whoever accepts me accepts the one who sent me" (John 13:19,20).

The right to ask for things in the name of Jesus is part of our delegated authority. So is the right to preach and minister in his name. We are empowered to represent Jesus on earth— to use his delegated power, his *exousia.* That's a lot of power! But *dunamis* adds more.

DUNAMIS: AUTHORITY ON THE INSIDE

When Jesus promised the disciples "power when the Holy Spirit comes," he had already given them *exousia.* Now he would add a power which would indwell them—inherent power.

When the Holy Spirit descended the day of Pentecost, the early Christians received the fullest measure of power possible for them (See Acts 2). They had *exousia* before, but now they also had *dunamis*—the full might of the Spirit himself living inside them. This power was manifest in miracles, prophecy, healing of the sick, and other compassionate deeds. These people were walking demonstrations that Jesus was alive. They were full of *chayil*.

The New Testament describes Christians in terms of the Holy Spirit inside of them. To be "in the Spirit," "full of the Spirit," "walking in the Spirit," "praying in the Spirit," and being a "temple of the Holy Spirit" were considered the norm for *all* believers. Their mission was to be "witnesses of Jesus Christ" (Acts 1:8). That mission was to be fulfilled by means of this supernatural power. As Paul put it in 1 Corinthians 2:4,5:

"My message and my preaching were not with wise and persuasive words, but with a demonstration of the Spirit's power, so that your faith might not rest on men's wisdom, but on God's power."

WAS DUNAMIS FOR WOMEN TOO?

On the day this power was first poured upon the church, women were full participants. Nobody could have any doubt about it.

"They all joined together constantly in prayer, along with *the women* and *Mary the mother* of Jesus, and his brothers" (Acts 1:14). (Italics mine.)

All of those 120—both men and women—began prophesying, praising God, and speaking in tongues when the Holy

Spirit arrived:

"All of them were filled with the Holy Spirit and began to speak in other tongues as the Spirit enabled them" (Acts 2:4). (Italics mine.)

Peter quoted a passage from Joel to explain the phenomenon. He was seeing a new spectacle: unusual public, vocal prophesying of women. He pointed out to the Jewish crowd:

"This is what was spoken by the prophet Joel:

"In the last days, God says, I will pour out my Spirit on all people. Your sons and *daughters* will prophesy, your young men will see visions, your old men will dream dreams.

"Even on my servants, *both men and women,* I will pour out my Spirit in those days, and they will prophesy" (Acts 2:16-18). (Italics mine.)

WOMEN PREACH THE GOSPEL

The presence of "prophesying women" was a natural part of life in the first-century church. Their preaching and powerful demonstration of miracles, healing, and authority over Satan dramatically influenced their world. When the Roman government began persecuting Christian preachers and leaders, many women were required to lay down their lives.

Both secular history and Scripture tell us about female leaders and teachers. For example, in Acts 21 we read of Philip's four daughters who prophesied. And the Corinthians asked Paul some questions about how women and men should dress when prophesying. In answering, he reiterated the non-exclusivity of prophecy:

"For you can *all* prophesy" (1 Cor. 14:31).

"Follow the way of love and eagerly desire spiritual gifts, especially the gift of prophecy" (1 Cor. 14:1).

"I would like *every one* of you to speak in tongues, but I would rather have you prophesy. He who prophesies is greater than one who speaks in tongues, unless he interprets, so that the church may be edified" (1 Cor. 14:5).

"Since you are eager to have spiritual gifts, try to excel in gifts that build up the church" (1 Cor. 14:12). (Italics mine.)

Such exhortations about prophecy appear often in the New Testament. In none of them is there any indication that women were excluded. Rather we see reference to the leadership of Prisca, Phoebe, Junia, and other women. These are included almost casually, as though there was nothing unusual about it.

IS POWER FEMININE?

Spirit-filled women are powerful women—persons of strength, might, authority, and ability. But is it feminine to be powerful? Some of us still wonder.

Turn the question around. Is it feminine to feign weakness and pretend helplessness? Isn't that an insult to God? A denial of the gift he has given us?

As Christians, we have been given two kinds of power: *exousia,* delegated authority, and *dunamis*—authority on the inside. *Dunamis* comes with the filling of the Holy Spirit. Inherent power is ours as we live as servants of God's kingdom on earth. In no way does it make us *less* of a woman. As we accept it as ours and live as a powerful person, we become *more* the woman God has always intended.

Ordinary Women—Extraordinary Strength

FOR YOUR OWN BIBLE STUDY

Two New Testament Words for "Power"

    dunamis—"inherent power, capability, ability to perform"

    exousia—"delegated authority, the right to exercise power"

1. *Dunamis* as translated in the New International Version:

Mark 5:30—"power"	Romans 15:19—"power"
Mark 6:2,5—"miracles"	1 Cor. 2:4-5—"power"
Luke 6:19—"power"	Col. 1:11,29—"power"
Acts 1:8; 4:7—"power"	"powerfully"

2. *Exousia* as translated in the New International Version:

Matt. 10:1—"authority"	John 1:12—"the right"
Luke 9:1; 10:19—"authority"	

3. Examples of *exousia* ("power of attorney," authority to act in Jesus' name):

John 13:19-20	John 16:23-24

4. *Dunamis* given to women:

Acts 1:14	Acts 2:16-18
Acts 2:4	John 13:19,20

5. *Women Receiving Power*

Acts 1:14, 2:4,16-18

6. *Note:*

One other Greek word was sometimes used as equivalent to the Hebrew *chayil*. It was also occasionally used as a synonym for *dunamis*. It is the word *arete,* often translated excellent or virtuous, meaning strong in character or quality. When Jesus spoke to the woman with the issue of blood, he asked who touched him, for he felt *"arete* go out from him." English Bibles translate this as virtue or power.

The Proverbs 31 woman could be said to include both *arete* and *dunamis,* of course, since her character and inner goodness were as much a part of her strength as any outward qualities.

Arete
Translated "virtue"
Phil. 4:8   2 Peter 1:3,5

Chapter 8

Chapter 8

Strength in Weakness

I had nothing to give. In fact, I had less than nothing. Rated on a scale of one to ten, my resources were around minus fifty. But the distraught man and woman who sat in my office insisted: *"God told us to come see you."*

My tired mind could not produce an alternative for them. It couldn't even formulate the proper words, which probably would be something like, "Can we set up an appointment for tomorrow?" Besides, I knew I would be no more ready to see them tomorrow. In a state of emotional burnout, I struggled with health problems and internal conflicts. I considered it a miracle each time I made it through another day.

I had hoped to be asleep two hours ago, I thought to myself as I sat quietly listening. *They must be able to tell I'm a basket case myself. Any moment now, they'll realize this is not God's woman of faith and power.*

Since I was too tired, too hopeless to attempt any problem solving or wise counsel, I gave the one thing I could give—a listening ear. What a tangled mess they had created for themselves. No wonder they were both at the breaking point. No wonder the crisis of their pain was so intense they couldn't wait until morning.

An hour of tearful unburdening ended, punctuated mostly by silence on my part. Then something beautiful happened that caught me completely off guard. All three of us felt it, and we knew God had intervened. Call it grace. Call it healing. I couldn't explain it, but suddenly, instantaneously everything was different.

They didn't request it, but I prayed with them before they left. We had nothing to ask for, only thanks for what God had just done. Two joyous people walked out—no, three joyous people walked out. In the middle of my weakness, possibly *because* of my weakness, God had let me participate in a miracle.

Less than a week later, I received a letter thanking me for what "I had done." They wrote: "From that night on, the world has been a different place. Next morning, it seemed the sky was blue again, the birds were singing. We are both completely healed and stand in amazement it could happen so quickly. We can never thank you enough. God knew what he was doing when he told us to come to you."

This experience was a watershed event for me and permanently changed my view of ministry. In a sense, it altered my relationship with God when it came to his "using" me. (Using is not what God does with us; using is what Playboy and Hugh Hefner do with women, and it is what Satan does with his victims. Since we are not tools, but beloved children, what God does is allow us to *participate* with him in the joyous and wonderful work of healing.)

After this experience, which came at an extremely low time for me, I truly understood why Paul could say, "for when I am weak, then I am strong" (2 Cor. 12:10).

That quote always sounded like a contradiction to me; or like a disclaimer from a person who wanted to be lazy, helpless, and powerless; or like a spiritual-sounding excuse for passivity, for taking no action, for copping out on responsible living.

Now I saw it in a different light. I understood that the power of the Holy Spirit was present in me whether I *felt* strong or not. My feelings of inadequacy in no way diminished his power. He can "use" me in my weakness.

He is not up in heaven biting his nails, impatient for Barbara to get strong so he can get on with the important work he has for her to do. God does not whisper nagging hints in my ear; "If you'd just get your act together, I'd let you do something for me today." Or, "Why don't you hurry up and get back to 'normal' so you can minister again?"

WHAT IS NORMAL?

The other day I talked with Kara, a young mother who has endured several major surgeries in the past few years. At far too young an age, she is grappling with a reality best described by Jesus when he said, "The spirit is willing, but the body is weak" (Matt. 26:41).

"How do I get closer to God?" she asked. "I want to be a strong Christian woman who has her life together, a good wife and mother."

That's what she wants or at least thinks she wants. But her energy runs out before her day does. She feels like a failure to God, defeated by the devil.

In this instance, I did have something to offer: "Relax. God is as close to you right now as he will ever be. Quit striving and let him love you. Give your body and emotions a chance to restore themselves.

"It's okay to be weak. It's even okay to be dependent on others for a time. Don't frustrate yourself trying to attain 'normal.' It's not what you think it is anyway. Your new 'normal' may be something very unlike your old 'normal.' So why worry about it? Leave all that up to God, and be who you are right now, a weak but loved wife and mother who is giving God a chance to work in her body and life."

Kara smiled with relief. "That's all?" she asked.

Jesus spoke to women like Kara:

"Come to me, all you who are weary and burdened, and I will give you rest. Take my yoke upon you and learn from me, for I am gentle and humble in heart, and you will find rest for your souls. For my yoke is easy and my burden is light" (Matt. 11:28-30).

WHO ARE THE WEAK?

Is his book, *The Strong and the Weak,* Paul Tournier, noted Swiss psychiatrist, looks at the ways God talks about people who are weak and how the Bible views the strong. In his opinion, who are the weak? Who are the strong? Which category includes us? Both. We are all weak, and we are all strong. New Christians are strong, but they are at the same time weak. Mature saints (wherever and whoever they may be) are strong in some ways and weak in other ways. The clergy, the businesswoman, the banker, the lawyer, the office supervisor, the carpool mother—none is exempt from occasions of weakness. Those of us who think we're an exception, one of those rare birds who fit exclusively in the "strong" category, just need to live a little longer. We shouldn't be surprised when we experience weakness, when we discover we are part of the human race after all. We mustn't let that discovery threaten our self-worth. God accepted us with no delusions; he never believed he was getting Wonder Woman.

LOSS OF STRENGTH

My husband, a strong robust man who played racquet ball three times a week, took long bike trips with me, skied and played golf (all on the same day, we used to joke) was stricken on his forty-fifth birthday with a serious heart attack. In a few hours, he went from strong to weak. He was so weak he was unable to do the most trivial things for himself: shave, brush his teeth, even read the get well cards.

"I feel so helpless, so useless," he moaned, "Lying here watching all these people wait on me."

Accustomed to serving others, it was a new experience to be the one in need. His reactions are typical of persons who are generally strong. It's a rude awakening and not at all pleasant to find out what weakness feels like.

"Trying to be strong" was not the right thing for him to do. In fact, it could have been fatal. His condition was so precarious that making polite conversation with a visitor would set off the heart monitoring machines. This was not the time to think spiritual thoughts like, "How can I minister to these nurses and doctors hovering around me?" I often told him, "It's okay to be weak. Helplessness is not failure."

Jerry responded to this crisis with admirable courage. He chose to rest in God and trust him. And if anyone can gain benefits from a miserable heart attack, he certainly did. One of the things he gained is an appreciation for helplessness. He discovered the value of being on the receiving end of ministry.

Nothing is wrong with being in need, nor is it a failure to admit we are weak and in need of others.

THE VALUE OF HELPLESSNESS

Recognition of our helplessness brings most of us to God. Accepting Jesus Christ as our Savior is an admission that we are helpless to save ourselves. If it's going to be done, God will have to do it.

Helen Reddy can sing, "I am strong, I am woman, I am invincible," but that song will never be her ticket into heaven. If we possessed what it takes to write our own ticket into eternal life, we wouldn't need Christ.

If we were as self-sufficient as Shirley MacLaine professes and could create our own reality and determine our own destiny, then, of course, we could conveniently ignore God. Possessed of such unfailing strength, we could afford to be arrogant. We would actually believe we had the right to decide right and wrong, create our own religion to fit our own needs, create "truth" out of our own mind.

What a frightening possibility. Thank God, it's not that way. Thank God, he created us strong, but not omnipotent.

Contemplating my human strengths will not move me to admit my need for God even though he is the One who gave me those strengths and talents. Whatever beauty is found inside you, whatever love, wisdom, or skills he has given generously for you to enjoy, will not draw you to him. It is your human weakness that will cause you to wonder, "Is there a God who cares for me? Is there someone out there bigger than me? A wisdom better than that of my limited brain?"

Our discussion of our strength as Christian women is not to be confused with mere positive self-talk. It's not an effort to psyche us up like a coach's locker-room pep talk. Positive talk by itself can be misleading. Positive confession is certainly better than the alternative (complaining), but it is unbalanced when left by itself.

STRENGTH RECOGNIZES HUMAN FRAILTY

Real strength, such as we have depicted, does not need to ignore our weakness as human beings. Its very beginning comes from admitting that we are not God. We are created beings. We stand in need of a Person greater than ourselves.

We acknowledge that we are, in all our God-given freedom and individual uniqueness, responsible to someone. We bow at his feet, humbly giving the worship due him and receiving his abilities to live our lives. We have not earned his gifts; we cannot claim we deserve his favor; but we believe he wants to have a relationship with us.

Through Jesus Christ, he has done for us what we were unable to do for ourselves; namely, handle the atonement for our sins. Now, our part is to receive God's gift as our own. "Saving faith," said Paul Tillich, "is having the courage to accept acceptance from God."

If our Christian faith begins with an awareness of our weaknesses, then what about its continuation? Some of us think it's okay to be weak *before* accepting Christ, but *after*...well, that's another story. Anticipating such misunderstanding, the Scripture says,

"Did you receive the Spirit by observing the law, or by *believing* what you heard? Are you so foolish? After beginning with the Spirit, are you now trying to attain your goal by human effort?" (Gal. 3:2,3).

DENIAL AND PLAY-ACTING

It's hard work to keep up the "strong-Christian-woman image." If strong means we must conceal our human failings, ordinary emotions, and bad days, then we have walked into a prison little better than the one occupied by the woman who believes she must be fragile and weak.

True strength is not play-acting, nor is it denial. It sees my weaknesses and embraces them, just as God does. During the journey between here and heaven, our weaknesses may not all be erased. But we need not run from them or fear to face them. Our weaknesses are as valuable as our strengths, because they constantly show us our need for God.

Paul talked much about weakness in Second Corinthians, an emotional letter in which he lays bare his own struggles. He wrote it during a stressful, painful time. He wrote from the awkward position of defending his right to minister.

His constant enemies, the Judaizers, followed him around using every propaganda technique known to the most power-hungry, unscrupulous politician. Smear campaigns, mudslinging, slander, libel, guilt by association, twisting his words—they did it all. And successfully. People believed them.

Because he had founded the Corinthian church, this was especially painful to Paul. "After all, you may have ten thousand teachers in the Christian faith, but you cannot have many fathers! For in Christ Jesus I am your spiritual father through the gospel" (1 Cor. 4:15 Phillips). He felt betrayed by their rejection.

WHAT A WIMP!

Some of his accusers hit at his being too human, too weak.

Taking advantage of his openness, they insisted a true apostle would be a stronger man, a more dominant person, in control at all times. "See! This wimp is no apostle!" they chided.

Others tried to find cracks in his armor by pointing out mistakes or supposedly unkept promises. Some Judaizers insulted his education and intelligence, although by any standard, including today's, he possessed keen intelligence and was highly trained in the best universities.

Another crowd cried, "Let's dump Paul. We're tired of him. We want a younger, more dynamic and good-looking leader. Someone who has a better television image." Some thought he was a terrible preacher: his stuff too weighty, too boring. Handsome Apollos with the silver tongue was far more interesting. Some of Paul's critics went as far as to insist he was an all out phony, just in it for the money.

REJECTION AND BETRAYAL

This kind of press doesn't contribute to one's self-esteem, especially when it is accepted as fact by the very people thought to be loyal friends. Paul was in much the same position as the man asked by reporters, "Have you stopped beating your wife yet?"

In the middle of this crisis in his ministry, the apostle says, "When I am weak, then I am strong." Let's look at that statement in context. After mentioning visions and revelations he had received (important credentials to some of his accusers) Paul told them:

> I am proud of an experience like that, but I have made up my mind not to boast of anything personal, except of my weaknesses. If I should want to boast I should certainly be no fool, for I should be speaking nothing

121

but the truth. Yet, I am not going to do so, for I don't want anyone to think more highly of me than is warranted by what he sees of me and hears from me (2 Cor. 12:5,6 Phillips).

He goes on to mention his thorn in the flesh, a messenger of Satan, and his appeal to God to remove it.

But his reply has been, 'My grace is enough for you: for where there is weakness, my power is shown the more completely.' Therefore, I have cheerfully made up my mind to be proud of my weaknesses, because they mean a deeper experience of the power of Christ. I can even enjoy weaknesses, insults, privations, persecutions and difficulties for Christ's sake. For my very weakness makes me strong in him (2 Cor. 12:8-10 Phillips).

A PRICELESS TREASURE

Paul is restating a point he made earlier in this same letter:

This priceless treasure we hold, so to speak, in common earthenware—to show that the splendid power of it belongs to God and not to us. We are hard-pressed on all sides, but we are never frustrated; we are puzzled, but never in despair. We are persecuted, but we never have to stand it alone: we may be knocked down, but we are never knocked out (2 Cor. 4:7-9 Phillips).

Is it any wonder this man prevailed? His stubborn hold on his source of power kept him preaching the gospel of grace in spite of all the discouragement. Paul's ministry is an inspiration to me. He was able to distinguish between human standards of competence and the competence God gives.

Thrown against varying human yardsticks, we will fall short at times. Someone strong is needed for a job and we feel "Weak. Very weak!" That's when we remind ourselves that our competence to minister comes only from God. I may feel up to it or quite unprepared. Either way, my competence comes from the same Source. God enables me, makes me adequate for the need. When I am weak, even then I am strong.

FOR YOUR OWN BIBLE STUDY
  Matthew 11:28-30
  Acts 18:24
  1 Corinthians 2:1,4,8
  1 Corinthians 9:4-14
  2 Corinthians (entire book)
  Galatians 3:2-5

Chapter 9

The Silent Strong

Shelley Brown sat next to her mother in the Sunday service, listening attentively to the sermon. Often the Scriptures her pastor shared answered questions surfacing in her mind.

Shelley's mother, appreciating a point in the sermon, leaned over and whispered a few agreeing words to her friend, Gwen.

The pastor stopped preaching, glared at the two women and shouted, "The Bible says women are to be silent in the church! Stop your rebellion this minute!"

"Is he talking to us?" whispered Mrs. Brown's friend.

The pastor's face grew red. "Ladies, I warn you!" Then he quoted from 1 Corinthians 14:37. 'What I [speak] to you is the Lord's command.' You had better obey me!"

Shelley walked out of the service in protest, never to return.

In her words, "I couldn't sit and do nothing when my mother was insulted. I want nothing to do with a church that quotes the Bible to justify prejudice against women."

ERRONEOUS BELIEFS

Although Shelley's experience is not an everyday event, ideas about the "proper place of women" *are common* and many have misunderstood the verse Mrs. Brown's pastor referred to.

At first glance, it presents a real problem. To us this sounds like a blunt put-down.

> Women should remain silent in the churches. They are not allowed to speak, but must be in submission, as the Law says. If they want to inquire about something, they should ask their own husbands at home; for it is disgraceful for a woman to speak in the church (1 Cor. 14:34,35).

WAS PAUL A CHAUVINIST?

Is it true, as some suggest, that the apostle Paul was a male chauvinist? Did he command all women to be silent or in subjection to men? Did he preach that women were inferior, gullible, unfit to teach or lead?

Those who accuse Paul of chauvinism base their opinions mainly upon two phrases of Scripture: 1 Timothy 2:12, "I do not permit a woman to teach" and the passage quoted above.

One secular writer used 1 Corinthians 11:7-9 as proof that the Bible is against women:

> For a man...is the image and glory of God; but the

128

woman is the glory of the man. For the man is not come of the woman, but the woman of the man, neither was the man created for the woman, but the woman for the man (KJV).

This writer said, "Imagine children reading or hearing this for the first time. And then think of all the incarnations of the female served up to them by the world's great religions. Woman, created by the He God *from* man and *for* man, is forever defined by her relationship to man."[1]

Are they right about the Christian faith? Do we worship a God who hates women? No, we do not. Nor was Paul prejudiced against women.

JUMPING TO CONCLUSIONS

Drawing conclusions about a person from only a small part of his writing is not wise. We cannot isolate a few sentences from Paul's letters and build whole doctrines out of them. We could take two sentences out of a dozen letters from a friend and use those to prove her prejudice against—say children or Southerners or Mexican-Americans. But fairness demands we read *all* that the friend has said about a subject (and consider the way she lives) before we draw conclusions.

Paul had much to say to women and about women in his letters. He had many female friends and coworkers. He wrote as if he respected them. Following is a list of passages where he spoke of women. A careful reading will show they were not statements designed to keep women "in their place." Taken *as a whole,* Paul's writings reveal just the opposite.

REFERENCES TO WOMEN IN PAUL'S LETTERS:

Romans	2 Corinthians	1 Timothy
1:26,27	11:1-3	2:8-10

4:18-21		2:11-15
7:1-3	**Galatians**	3:1,2
9:6-13	3:28	3:11
9:25	4:4,5	5:1,2
16:1,2	4:21-31	5:3-16
16:3-5		
16:6	**Ephesians**	**2 Timothy**
16:12	5:21-23	3:6,7
16:13	6:1-3	4:19
16:15		4:21
1 Corinthians	**Philippians**	**Titus**
1:10,11	4:2,3	1:5,6
6:15,16		2:3-5
7:1-5	**Colossians**	
7:8-11	3:18,19	**Philemon**
7:25-40	3:20	2
9:3-5	4:15	
11:2-16		
14:33-36	**1 Thessalonians**	
16:19	2:7,8	
	4:3-8	

This list shows a minimum number of passages we must read in their context before we can draw conclusions about Paul's attitude toward women. When we take a close look, we find that Paul was, more than any leader except Christ, a friend to women.[2]

DID PAUL FORGET?

How could this same apostle write such a thing as "Let the women be silent in the churches?" Did he forget all he had said earlier?

As we come to know Paul through his writings, we find it hard to believe he would deliberately contradict himself in 1 Timothy 2:12 and 1 Corinthians 14:34. It is equally impossible to believe that the Holy Spirit, in choosing Paul as the human instrument for setting down Scripture, allowed him to make mistakes in all other passages but these two.

The problems lie with our understanding. Our preconceptions and mental blocks cause us to focus on one piece of data which *seems* to establish a command. These preconceptions blind us to the fact that the command would cancel out the intent of the book in which it appears.

Sometimes we are like the Pharisees. Even though God spoke to them face to face in the person of Jesus, they tried to bend his words to fit their system. Laws and customs were their security blanket. They didn't like anybody challenging those customs. Their customs included, by the way, countless little regulations which kept women "in their place." As we read through the Gospels, we see Jesus deliberately ignoring these rules in order to minister to women.

JESUS' ATTITUDE

This brings us to another question. What was Jesus' attitude and behavior toward women? Few people have summarized it better than Dorothy Sayers:

Perhaps it is no wonder that the women were first at the cradle and last at the Cross. They had never known a man like this Man—there never has been such another. A prophet and teacher who never nagged at them, never flattered or coaxed or patronized; who never made arch jokes about them, never treated them either as "The women, God help us!" or "The ladies, God bless

131

them!"; who rebuked without querulousness and praised without condescension; who took their questions and arguments seriously; who never mapped out their sphere for them, never urged them to be feminine or jeered at them for being female; who had no axe to grind and no uneasy male dignity to defend; who took them as he found them and was completely unself-conscious. There is no act, no sermon, no parable in the whole gospel that borrows its pungency from female perversity; nobody could possibly guess from the words and deeds of Jesus that there was anything "funny" about woman's nature.[3]

If we skim through the Gospels we can quickly note Jesus' attitude toward women. For example, in John 4:1-42, we find his conversation with the woman at the well; in Luke 8:40-48, the woman who had an issue of blood. Luke 7:36-39 describes the woman who washed Jesus' feet with her tears.

In each of these instances, Jesus ignored at least one of the Pharisees' laws: a rabbi was forbidden to speak with a woman in public, even if she was a relative. To be seen talking with a woman could taint his reputation. He could be labeled as flirtatious—or worse.

WOMEN IN THE SYNAGOGUES

When Jesus worshiped at the synagogue, the Jewish women were indeed "silent in the church." They had to hold their questions until they could ask their husbands. As traditions developed, Jewish leaders progressively excluded women from everything important. They were not allowed to participate in worship, in government, or in public life.

Little boys were carefully taught the Scriptures, but little girls were not. In fact, it was against local laws for a man to teach his daughter to read or allow her to study the Old Testament. (When Mary *learned* at Jesus' feet while her sister Martha cooked, she disobeyed the rules. Jesus also disobeyed them by teaching her.)

These customs never came from God. They are not found in the law of Moses nor in the prophets. But as time went on, the Jewish leaders forgot that their customs and the laws of God were two separate items. In any argument, the Pharisees had the last word: "The Bible says so," they declared.

THE BIBLE SAYS IT, I BELIEVE IT, THAT SETTLES IT

I once met a pastor who insisted that sex came into the world through the sin of Eve—a result of the fall. In other words, sexual relations between a man and a woman were not in God's plan. After Eve ate the forbidden fruit, she became evil and lustful. She invented sex to tempt God's noble man Adam and bring about his fall.

"Where do you find that in the Bible?" I asked, trying to remain congenial.

"Well, it says, 'Adam knew her not until Cain was conceived.'"

"Are you *sure* that's in the Bible?" I said. "Let's look."

Of course we found no such verse, though we carefully scrutinized every word of the first five chapters of Genesis.

"It's in there somewhere! I *know* that's what the Bible says," declared the pastor.

To this day I'm sure he preaches that women invented sin and every one of us is an incurable seductress. We feel continual lust and are always plotting to get power over men.

In a similar way, the Pharisees claimed scriptural backing for their regulations for women. They liked to end their speeches with the authoritative phrase, "as it says also in the law."

Who would dare disagree with the law? If it was in the book, that settled it. What commoner could risk asking, *"Where in the law do we find this custom?"* If a woman questioned the rule, she wasn't permitted to speak in public anyway.

JESUS CALLS THEIR BLUFF

Until Jesus, few had the audacity to challenge the officious Pharisees. They intimidated with their "knowledge" of the law. Jesus had an inside track; he knew that half their "as the law says" claims could not be validated—the law did *not* say it. Of course, they were furious when he pointed this out. Without an actual written command in the Scriptures, their customs were as phony as a Hollywood movie set. The exposure was humiliating.

Jesus didn't seem very polite when he talked to the Pharisees. He was rough on them; he sometimes called them snakes or whitewashed tombs full of dead men's bones. Not exactly the way to win friends and influence people. He let them know what he thought of their phony rules and so-called religion.

TRADITIONS NULLIFY JUSTICE

Quoting their best prophet, Jesus told these legalists:

Isaiah was right when he prophesied about you...'They worship me in vain; their teachings are but rules taught by men.'

You have let go of the commands of God and are holding on to the traditions of men....you nullify the word of God by your tradition (Mark 7:6,7,8,13).

How does all of this relate to women and the verse about their silence? In order to understand, we have to know how the people who first read it understood it.

Paul followed the example of Jesus in dealing with the Pharisees and their successors—Judaizers—legalists who wanted all Christians to live by Jewish customs. Because Jesus had made such a point of showing the difference between Jewish traditions and real godliness, Paul was adamant about the same issue. Because he had been a Pharisee himself (See Philippians 3:5), he understood their traditions.

RADICAL DECLARATION

Paul knew that Jesus crossed cultural and religious barriers to involve himself in the lives of women. He knew that Jesus ignored the rabbis' traditions and showed disregard for society's expectations of women.

On the subject of Gentiles and slaves, as well as women, Paul cut the cord with Jewish tradition when he drew his radical conclusion in Galatians 3:28, "There is neither Jew nor Greek, slave nor free, male nor female, for you are all one in Christ Jesus." If other strong statements had not already alienated him from the religious leaders, this one would have. The distinction between Jews and non-Jews was essential to their system. All the customs they held dear would be meaningless if they gave the same privileges to Gentiles as Jews, to women as men, to slaves as citizens.[4]

MOCKING THE PHARISEES

Paul followed the same tack as Jesus in challenging the Judaizers. Having excelled in the acts of Pharisaism himself, he knew how to hit hard at their weak points. He often made fun of them just as Jesus did. Paul might quote the Pharisees and in mock seriousness add, "as the law says," knowing perfectly well the law did *not* say. He describes their superior attitude and then goes on to poke fun:

"Did the word of God originate with you? Or are you the only people it has reached?" (1 Cor. 14:36).

This feature of Paul's writing must not be underestimated. He passionately fought the hold of Jewish traditionalism in the early church. He believed it an anti-gospel and therefore no gospel at all. He believed, as did Jesus, that the religious leaders, the "experts in the law...have taken away the key to knowledge" (Luke 11:52).

Jesus said to them, "You yourselves have not entered (the kingdom), and you have hindered those who were entering" (Luke 11:52). "You are like unmarked graves, which men walk over without knowing it" (Luke 11:44). Jesus made many such denunciating statements to the Pharisees. His apostle Paul was no different with the legalists a few years later.

TONE OF VOICE

To understand the tone in which Paul wrote, we need to picture him as the man who spoke with scathing denunciation of legalism, Pharisaism, and rabbinic traditions. We must picture him just as we picture Jesus in his "woe to you Pharisees" sermons. Otherwise, we can't make sense of some of his best dialogues. We will make commands of statements in which he quoted his enemies. Like quoting words from the mouths of Job's comforters or ascribing the devil's words to God, this is misuse of Scripture.

EMOTIONAL DIALOGUE

In First and Second Corinthians, Paul dealt with attitudes needing correction. He dialogued with the Corinthian believers, rephrasing their questions and answering them. Sometimes he described their immature attitudes, then ridiculed these attitudes. In his unique style of communication, Paul used wit, sarcasm, exhortation, and encouragement. He drew on his literary knowledge, quotes from Greek poets and philosophers, and illustrations from Old Testament history. He wrote emotionally, personally, humorously, and seriously. He displayed his own humanity with its strengths and weaknesses. He wrote of his feelings, struggles, doubts, and his glorious relationship with God.

We learn much about this interesting leader if we read at one sitting the two Corinthian letters. They are intense letters, displaying nearly the whole gamut of human emotions. When we come to the twelfth, thirteenth and fourteenth chapters, we see his impatience with their quarrels over spirituality. If we look closely, we see ourselves in these people and their problems.

MISUSING THE GIFTS

Paul is irate that the Corinthians have misused the manifestations of the Holy Spirit for reasons of competition, pride, and jealousy. He does not solve the problem by putting an end to the public use of these gifts. Nor does he contradict himself by saying, "Let's limit the prophesying to those of you who are Jews. You know the Old Testament." Or, "From now on, only those over age thirty-five will be allowed to prophesy. The rest of you are too young."

Nor did he say the participants in a Christian meeting should be restricted by sex, citizenship, or position. He knew that to handle the problems in these ways would contradict Galatians 3:28: "There is neither Jew nor Greek, slave nor free, male nor female, for you are all one in Christ Jesus."

ALL MAY PROPHESY

How did he solve these problems? In essence, he said, "You

may *all* prophesy. But use some common courtesy." His suggestions show us that Paul saw unique value in every member of the Corinthian church, whether male or female:

> To one there is given through the Spirit the message of wisdom, to another the message of knowledge by means of the same Spirit, to another faith by the same Spirit, to another gifts of healing by that one Spirit, to another miraculous powers, to another prophecy, to another distinguishing between spirits, to another the ability to speak in different kinds of tongues, and to still another the interpretation of tongues (1 Cor. 12:8-10).

> All these are the work of one and the same Spirit, and he gives them to each one, just as he determines (1 Cor. 12:11).

> But God has combined the members of the body and has given greater honor to the parts that lacked it, so that there should be no division in the body, but that its parts should have equal concern for each other (1 Cor. 12:24,25).

> What then shall we say, brothers? When you come together, everyone has a hymn, or a word of instruction, a revelation, a tongue or an interpretation. All of these must be done for the strengthening of the church (1 Cor. 14:26).

> For you can all prophesy in turn so that everyone may be instructed and encouraged (1 Cor. 14:31).

COURTESY AND CONSIDERATION

He concludes this discussion by emphasizing: "But everything should be done in a fitting and orderly way" (1 Cor. 14:40).

This discussion contains the verse about "silent women." In the paragraph just before his conclusion, we read one of Paul's sarcastic questions to those who presumed superspirituality:

"Did the word of God originate with you? Or are you the only people it has reached?" (1 Cor. 14:36).

His answer to these self-appointed holders of special revelation is:

If anybody thinks he is a prophet or spiritually gifted, let him acknowledge that what I am writing to you is the Lord's command. If he ignores this, he himself will be ignored (1 Cor. 14:37,38).

What was he so upset about? What had been their special revelation? What "word of God" were they claiming to have originated?

The preceding comments reveal what angered him: an attitude toward women which obviously came from the Judaizers. Their language is recognizable here:

Women should remain silent in the churches. They are not allowed to speak, but must be in submission, *as the Law says*. If they want to inquire about something, they should ask their own husbands at home; for it is disgraceful for a woman to speak in the church (1 Cor.

14:34,35). (Italics mine.)

WHAT LAW?

Notice "as the Law says." Paul would never appeal to Jewish law as the basis for Christian behavior. If he had, he'd use a law which could be found. This law is non-existent. The law of Moses said nothing about silence for women, nor did the Roman law of Corinth.

The only law which restricted women in worship was *Jewish custom*—the oral law of *tradition*. This is the very practice Jesus denounced when he accused the Pharisees of substituting man-made rules for God's laws.

The Jews believed it was disgraceful for a woman to speak in church. Paul disagreed. He encouraged all believers to share their gifts to build up the body of Christ and preach the gospel in the world.

In Jewish synagogues women were silent, passive observers. They listened to the men read the Scriptures, listened to the men pray, listened as the men worshiped. They were not even allowed to sit with their husbands. They were relegated to the women's gallery.

NO MORE SEGREGATION

Rabbis told the women to be silent during worship. No matter how bored, they were not to whisper or talk among themselves. They were to reverently watch the men's magnificent performance in awe and wonder. If they didn't understand what was read or preached, they shouldn't discuss it with each other. Another woman would be too ignorant to have a sensible answer. "Let them ask their husbands," said the rabbis. "And please, ladies, wait until you get home to do so."

Some Jewish believers expected Christian meetings to carry

140

on in the same pattern. The Judaizers did not see any need to change "the way we've always done it."

It is not surprising that one of the arguments in Corinth revolved around the "place of women." Should women be allowed to prophesy? To speak in *public*? To pray right out loud in the presence of men?

Remember it all started in a flamboyant way—this business of women speaking publicly. It happened on the day of Pentecost. Peter and the other disciples were dyed-in-the-wool Jewish men; but when they heard the women prophesy and speak in tongues that day, they recognized it was scriptural. The prophet Joel had predicted it would happen.

Paul was adamant about ending the restrictions on women. He poured the full force of his satire on these so-called experts in the law. "As the law says? Oh really? What law? Where in the Bible do you find it? Show me."

Knowing they could never produce a reference, he pulled the curtain on their phony expertise, letting them know he was aware that their "law" on silencing women was a mere human fabrication. "You made up this law! You and the long line of rabbis before you. Who do you think you are? The originators of the word of God?"

He brought them to this conclusion: "If a man is truly spiritual, he will acknowledge that the instructions I have set down in this letter are the command of God. And those who ignore me? Here's how to handle them in the future...ignore them! Take no stock in what they tell you. We're done living by their useless laws!"

THE ANGRY ENEMY

Were the law lovers angry with Paul? You bet they were! Many left the church.

Ordinary Women—Extraordinary Strength

What happened to the women? They were released to preach, pray, prophesy, and minister in Corinth and other cities.

On the walls of the catacombs in Rome, the early Christians left records of their life together. Drawings and engravings depict scenes from their worship and meetings. In many of these scenes, a woman is shown preaching or leading the meeting.

History tells us that many early women preachers became martyrs. It's possible that as many women were arrested by the Roman government as men. Their crime? Preaching the gospel of Jesus Christ and causing so many people to follow him.

Are women to be silent in churches?

Never again!

FOR YOUR OWN BIBLE STUDY
References to women in Paul's letters, pages 129, 130.

Chapter 10

Chapter 10

Can Women Teach and Preach?

Let's turn our attention to the other puzzling passage for women.

I also want women to dress modestly, with decency and propriety, not with braided hair or gold or pearls or expensive clothes, but with good deeds, appropriate for women who profess to worship God.

A woman should learn in quietness and full submission. I do not permit a woman to teach or to have authority over a man; she must be silent. For Adam was formed first, then Eve. And Adam was not the one deceived; it was the woman who was deceived and became a sinner (1 Tim. 2:9-14).

So! We can't teach, can't wear gold or pearls or braid our hair. We must be silent besides. At first glance, it may look as if that's what we're to think.

Remember we can't ignore the rest of the Bible. We have demonstrated that the Bible does not contradict itself. We have gained enough understanding of Paul to help us see why he wrote these words to Timothy. Let's take a look at some facts we already know.

Many women did teach in first century churches. These women preached publicly with no opposition from the apostles unless they taught false doctrines. The apostles opposed anyone, male or female, who dealt in false doctrine. This is important to remember when we read First and Second Timothy because Paul wrote those books to a young pastor dealing with some serious heresies. Nearly a third of each letter is Paul's attempt to correct these heresies.

Paul worked closely with women in the ministry. He took Priscilla and Aquila to Ephesus to teach in the church. (See Acts 18:18,19) We know from early church history of the many women imprisoned and martyred for preaching Christ. Their persecution came, not from Peter or Paul, but from the Roman government. Jewish religious leaders and Judaizers, fussing about their laws and traditions, also fired criticism at women leaders.

USURPING AUTHORITY

Hundreds of years ago, well meaning theologians decided the passage was a prohibition, not against women teaching, but against women teaching *men*. If a woman were to teach a group in which men were present, she was "usurping authority."

This was the real sin; any woman who taught Scripture in

the presence of a man, even her husband or brother, stole a position that only a male could rightly hold. She was usurping—stealing his leadership rights. Teaching is a form of leadership and only males have the right to lead, they said.

This line of reasoning maintained that the prohibition was meant to protect the church from error. Women should not preach doctrine or theology because, in their susceptibility to Satan's deception, they could lead the whole church into heresy. Noting, however, that women *were* admonished to teach in Titus 2:2-5, these theologians admitted women might be allowed to teach other women and children.

PROTECT MEN BUT NOT CHILDREN

A friend of ours was having a little fun with his fellow preachers. "So you don't believe women should be allowed to teach the word. Let me ask. Who are the Sunday school teachers in your church? How many of them are female? What? *All* of them? Then aren't you practicing a terrible contradiction to your beliefs?"

"Oh, no! We're very scriptural. These Sunday school classes are for children. Women can teach the word to children."

"Now you're telling me you're not only prejudiced against women, you're showing me you also have a rotten attitude toward children."

Aren't women and children part of the body of Christ? Can a theologian believe it doesn't matter what heresy is taught the children of a church? Or the women? Just so the men aren't exposed to false teaching?

YOU OUGHT TO BE TEACHERS

These interpretations, usually based on one or two proof texts, can only be accepted if we close our eyes to the rest of Scripture. About teaching the word, for example, the writer of Hebrews says:

> We have much to say about this, but it is hard to explain because you are slow to learn. In fact, though by this time *you ought to be teachers,* you need someone to teach you the elementary truths of God's word all over again. You need milk, not solid food (Heb. 5:11,12)! (Italics mine.)

The tone is scolding. These believers should have learned enough by now to be effectively teaching the word. No hint is given that all the believers addressed were male. We cannot presume that women were excluded from those who "ought to be teachers."

WOMEN IN AUTHORITY

What about the question of women having authority over men? Why this reminder of who was created first? Does it imply that being created first makes a person an automatic ruler over the one created second?

Is this the original male chauvinist speaking? "Hey, girls! We were here first. That makes us smarter. Besides, your ancestor, Eve—she was deceived, remember? Eve was taken in. She became a sinner, you know. This makes you a second class citizen. Anyone can figure it out: the one created first is obviously supposed to rule the ones created second and third."

Imagine a conversation like this with Paul. He stands in his long Jewish robes, a scroll in hand, his eyes staring intently. We feel smugly delighted after he makes this last point. Aha! Now we have him. "That's great reasoning!" we say.

"Now you've proven that the animals have authority over men."

This scenario is, of course, impossible. As we've seen in earlier chapters, Paul was a lot smarter than that.

Look at the passage in its entire context:

> I want men everywhere to lift up holy hands in prayer, without anger or disputing.
>
> I also want women to dress modestly, with decency and propriety, not with braided hair or gold or pearls or expensive clothes, but with good deeds, appropriate for women who profess to worship God.
>
> A woman should learn in quietness and full submission. I do not permit a woman to teach or to have authority over a man; she must be silent. For Adam was formed first, then Eve. And Adam was not the one deceived; it was the woman who was deceived and became a sinner. But women will be kept safe through childbirth, if they continue in faith, love and holiness with propriety (1 Tim. 2:8-15).

The phrases hardest to understand are:
1. "A woman should learn in quietness and full submission."
2. "I do not permit a woman to teach or to have authority over a man; she must be silent."
3. "For Adam was formed first, then Eve."

LITERAL COMMANDMENTS?

If this is a list of literal commands for all time, then we must be consistent in applying *all* of them *to both men and women.* Suppose we decided to practice them as rules in our churches:

1. A man would be allowed to pray *only* with his hands raised.
2. Men would not be allowed to pray if they had harbored anger, behaved angrily, or been involved in an argument.
3. Women would not be allowed to wear gold or pearls in any form, including watches and rings. (Costume jewelry might be acceptable. And, of course, we could probably get by with plastic jewelry, turquoise, diamonds, silver, and rubies.)
4. Braided hairstyles would be banned, including those of little girls.
5. Women would learn in church, but in silence.
6. Women would not be allowed to teach, Sunday school included.
7. Women would not be elected to any leadership offices, including Sunday school, choir, and church committees if men or boys were part of the group. This leaves only the women's missionary society or women's prayer group.
8. Women would be silent observers to worship, not allowed to sing, pray, speak, or converse.

Most of us would not be willing to attend a church like that. Men would not like it any more than we women would. What did this passage mean to the original hearers? *Why* did Paul say these specific things to Timothy in Ephesus?

PROBLEMS OF A YOUNG CHURCH

In the first sentences of First Timothy, we are told that Timothy was put in Ephesus for a specific assignment, "so that you may command certain men not to teach false doctrines any longer nor to devote themselves to myths and endless genealogies" (1 Tim. 1:3,4).

Heresies were beginning in Ephesus. Some of the heretics focused attention on religious women. They promoted a female priesthood which claimed *superior* authority and power *over men.* Much of Paul's advice had to do with the heresies and myths and the problems they caused.

MYTHS AND LEGENDS

Raised with myths and legends, many Ephesian Christians had been sold on the serpent as the source of knowledge. Others revered Eve as someone who wisely aligned with the serpent so she could receive "deeper truth" and the "mysteries of the universe."

These heresies never disappeared. They have resurfaced recently in our country, hardly bothering to change clothes. As in Ephesus, these heresies are accepted by sophisticated people, some of them famous and wealthy. Many are eager to present their deeper truths on television talk shows. They will even demonstrate their "channeling" abilities for the viewer to see.

GODDESSES AND SEX

The Ephesian Christians lived in a licentious environment. If we think American pornography is bad, we'd have been even more shocked by a tour of ancient Ephesus. We wouldn't want to raise our children there.

Ephesus was the site of the world-famed temple of Artemis (Diana). In addition, it boasted the temple of Aphrodite (also called Venus the harlot). The worship of Artemis and Aphrodite was part of a long tradition of goddesses who served as mediators between earth and heaven. This was accomplished through religious rites of sexual intercourse with the priestess. To the Ephesians, spirituality had something to do with sex.

SACRED MARRIAGE

Had we been among the thousands who worshiped Artemis or Aphrodite in Ephesus, we would have participated in "sacred marriage."

"Sacred marriage...enacted by...priest and priestess or by sacred prostitute and worshiper, effected a union with the god, bringing salvation and fertility. The cult prostitutes constituted a significant proportion of the Ephesian population. The office of temple courtesan, whether temporary or permanent, was considered commendable, as is evidenced by inscriptions proclaiming the piety of those who had served in this manner."[1]

No wonder Paul reminded Timothy, "there is one God and *one mediator* between God and men, the man Christ Jesus" (1 Tim. 2:5). The Ephesians needed to learn that no channelers were needed.

FASHIONS OF VENUS

Religious women were sexy women. The temples provided the priestesses with the finest designer wardrobes Paris could supply. (Well, their *haute couture* probably came from Egypt, the then-fashion capital for seductive women.) Pearls and gold plus flashy and expensive clothes were necessary to an appropriate public image for a priestess of Venus, the love goddess. Braided hair was considered alluring, so her hair was arranged in braids.

The priestess was identifiable in the city streets as one of the "spiritual" women. Everyone believed she possessed "deeper truth" through her devotion to Venus. Everything about her manner, voice, and appearance was carefully turned out as advertising for the temple. If she were effective, men would want to worship her goddess by joining their bodies to hers.

We can easily see how important it was that distinctions be extremely clear between Christian worship and traditional Ephesian worship, and between Christian women and pagan priestesses. Any Christian woman who took a visible role, teaching or prophesying, was likely to be labeled a "religious woman." In a city where "religious woman" also meant "sexually available woman," it would be difficult to communicate past the label. Extra measures were necessary in this situation.

DRESS WITH DIGNITY

When we understand that feature of life in Ephesus, it makes perfect sense to tell a pastor, "Ask your women to dress modestly, avoid the display of expensive clothes, jewelry, and braids in their hair."

Women who grew up in strict Jewish homes probably knew that women who worship God ought to dress decently and appropriately. Ephesian girls who came from pagan homes wouldn't necessarily know. Most of Timothy's congregation were born and raised right there in Ephesus. They had to be taught that a true spirituality was possible for women, one that did *not* include fornication. The church in Ephesus needed to show its city a new kind of woman—one with intrinsic value, not dependent on clothes or jewelry or sex appeal for her worth.

This woman had dignity. She wore clothing that showed her identity was not dependent on men's attentions. She behaved herself with serenity and grace in a culture where goddess worship had warped women's views of themselves, a culture where Venus and Diana controlled men's fantasies, attitudes towards women, and pocketbooks. (See Acts

19:23-31).

NEW WOMAN, NEW WARDROBE

I am offended if a church dictates the clothing of its women. In many parts of America, "clothesline Christianity" is a thing of the past, but it hasn't been long since women new to the church would be told, "No makeup, no jewelry, no nail polish," or given lists of approved clothing. Although I don't like it, at certain times in our years of pastoring, I have seen the logic behind such rules. Monique, for example:

Before she accepted Christ, Monique was a street prostitute. After she accepted Christ, she left the streets and became a part of the college-age group in our church. She enjoyed new friends, spiritual growth, and fun times with the group. She began gaining self-respect and getting her life together after such a painful past.

Monique confided excitedly, "I'm asking God to give me a Christian husband. Some day I'm going to have a happy family and a nice home. God is already giving me so many blessings, I know he'll do that for me, too."

However, the Christian men in the group didn't seem interested in a serious relationship with Monique. Not because of her past—few of them knew about it. Not because she was unattractive or obnoxious. She was well-liked and treated as a friend and sister.

"Every guy I date tells me he just wants to be a friend," she complained. "Why doesn't one of them want something more serious?"

She confided this complaint to the last of the long list who dated her and made the "friend" speech. His answer was gentle but honest. She told me about it with no hurt feelings, only gratitude that he had cared enough to be direct with her.

Mark told her, "Monique, if you want Christian men to take you seriously, you should quit looking like a street-walker. I mean, all that heavy make-up and the glitzy dresses that look like you're in a nightclub act—they're just not you. But guys believe the label. Get rid of those too-tight clothes and greasy green eyelids."

Remember, Mark had no knowledge that she had been a street-walker. He simply described what her clothes said about her. She was only too happy to make the small change in appearance that made a big difference in her future.

THE NEW WOMAN FOR TODAY

The strong woman we have depicted is our model. Adorned with the beautifying quality of love, she is not passive but active. She expresses her strength through what the Bible calls good works—deeds of kindness to others.

See the parallels in our own world. Doesn't the church of today need to display a new kind of woman?

FOR YOUR OWN BIBLE STUDY
   Isaiah 3:16-23
   Luke 2:36-38
   Acts 18:18,19
   Acts 19:23-31
   Acts 21:9
   1 Timothy 1:3,4
   1 Timothy 2:8-15
   Titus 2:2-5
   Hebrews 5:11,12
   1 Peter 3:3,4

Chapter 11

Religious Women and Misused Power

Smiling, hugging, and saying, "Praise the Lord, Brother," he made his way from the front door to a seat in the crowded room. Although it was his first time at the youth Bible study, he appeared to feel right at home. The group was warm, caring, loving. Some were dressed like him, in holey jeans and bare feet.

These people were excited about the Bible, too. No dry stuff here. They asked questions, made comments, and entered into lots of discussion. After the first fifteen minutes, he asked his own question.

"Who's the teacher here?" asked the new young man with the long pony tail.

"I'm the teacher," I replied, a little surprised he couldn't tell.

"The Bible says a woman is not supposed to teach the word of God. Right here in 1 Timothy 2:12 it says..." He proceeded to read the passage to us, emphasizing the part about my "usurping authority" over men.

CHICKS RAMBLE

Remarkably, I did not feel defensive as I listened. I let him go all the way through his little speech. At one point, I almost jumped in. That was when he explained that "chicks aren't able to think very clearly; and when they talk, they ramble off in all directions." I bit my tongue and held my peace, seeing the degree to which the anger thermostat of the group had climbed. At least two-thirds of the participants that day were men—big guys his age, and some of them not long removed from the streets. *I hope they're kind,* I thought. *If not, then I'll jump in.*

The remainder of the hour was delightful. I sat in silence and listened as my class "taught him the way more perfectly."

"In the first place," John replied, "Mrs. Cook was appointed the leader of this group by the Christian Education Board of our church. She's not usurping anything. Secondly, we're here because we want to be. Nobody makes us come to hear her teach."

"Yeah," chimed in Brad. "It's your choice. If you don't want a woman teacher, you don't have to come."

"Isn't that prejudice?" asked the saved civil rights protester. "How can you believe God only speaks through men? That's only half the human race he has to work with."

This reminded others of the great women described in the Bible as mightily used of God. They contributed Scripture readings about Miriam the prophetess, Deborah, Huldah, Sarah, and a few others. They they covered the New Testament, starting with the Spirit being poured out on women at the day of Pentecost.

Wondering whether he was suffering too badly, I watched our visitor intently. To all appearances, he was in shock. His eyes were wide open, his hands turning the pages, following each Scripture they read. When they ran down, nearly every man present having said his piece, the poor fellow spoke.

"Wow! Heavy, man!" (This event took place during the period in history known as the Jesus Movement. People talked like that then.) "I have really learned a lot today. You've like shown me the whole Bible, ya know. Like, man, I only knew there was one verse in there about chicks. I'm real new to all this Bible stuff. Thanks for teaching me."

SATISFYING YOURSELF

This was the first, therefore the best remembered, instance where I was questioned about my right to teach Scripture. Although the young men in our Bible study did a great job of defending my right to teach, the experience challenged me early on to thoroughly and painstakingly study the word for myself on this subject.

I had to be entirely convinced inside, with no shadow of doubt, if I were going to preach and teach God's word and know it was his will. In my studies, I ran across accounts of other women who faced the same need:

> It is incumbent upon Christian women to explain themselves. They profess obedience to the Word. They think that St. Paul forbade women teachers of the Bible. Yet they teach and pray and preach:...With women rests the responsibility to explain the Apostle Paul in a convincing manner, as not in opposition to their conduct...a woman who is called to preach is likewise called

to an understanding of the Word which will agree with that inward choice.[1]

Those words were written in 1919 by the famous preacher, Jessie Penn-Lewis. In another generation, she faced the challenge of defending her right to carry out the great commission. Even though she and many other powerful women of that generation successfully explained themselves and validated their calling, we of this generation have to do it all over again. We need to satisfy ourselves, so that, when we are challenged, we know in our hearts that *God* does not consider us "usurping" anything, even if some people do.

Our first clue to discovering which heresies troubled Ephesian women comes in the form of a strange Greek word used only once in the entire Bible. Paul's choice of that particular word in 2 Timothy 2:12 makes obvious the intent of his statement about women teaching and having authority.

A DIFFERENT WORD

What is meant by this phrase originally translated in the King James Version as usurping authority? What is this one word Paul used? It is not the usual word used for authority, not *dunamis* or *exousia*, not even one of the words the Greeks used for lead or rule. All those words are used for both men and women.

To explain the significance of this word and how it still has meaning for us today, we need to lay some groundwork. We need more knowledge of the heresies featuring religious women which threatened the early church. We also need to understand the heresies which ascribed wisdom to the serpent and superior knowledge to Eve.

The presence of these heresies occasioned many of the New Testament books to be written. The apostles had to explain how Christianity differed from these beliefs before the heretical ideas were stirred into the pot and passed down as part of the Christian faith.

WOMEN AND SEXUAL POWER

I saw a greeting card which featured only one word on the front in large letters: SEX. When opened, it read, "Now that I have your attention...."

We, too, will start with the part that has to do with sex. The word translated "usurp authority" in 1 Timothy 2:12 is the Greek word *authentein*. It has a lot to do with sex.

A certain kind of woman is seen in soap operas on T.V. Joan Collins has made a fortune playing one on a nighttime soap. Probably every daytime serial features at least one character of this type just to keep things interesting. She's the one we just hate. She's conniving, seductive, always plotting. She uses sex to get power over men. She allures, seduces, captures his heart, traps him, then has him where she wants him...totally at her mercy. When he least expects it, she suddenly draws her dagger, plunges the knife into his heart, and twists.

ABNORMAL CRAVING

This woman craves power—especially, for some neurotic reason, power over men. In her most depraved state, she hates men, all men, but pretends to love them. Her game is to use men, exploit men, wring them dry—of their love or money or whatever—then dump them in the most rejecting, humiliating way possible. Without at least a few of these women in modern America, there would be fewer sad songs for disc jockeys to play. Elvis could never have sung Heartbreak Hotel or Don't Be Cruel. And country western singers would be narrowed down to home, mother's prayers, and apple pie.

All the terms in our language describing this woman are obscene. Maybe that's as it should be, because this kind of woman is obscene. She is the woman who uses sex as a tool, a weapon. She knows the power it can wield, and she has become an expert in all the techniques of its use. She misuses herself, her charms, and her sexuality to gain dominion over a person. She wants complete control, possession, ownership.

RELIGIOUS WOMEN WERE DANGEROUS

The modern attitude toward this kind of woman is negative, disapproving, antagonistic. We've come a long way from the popular attitude that existed when the New Testament was written. In that day, these women were admired. They were prophetesses, priestesses, daughters of Eve, channels to deeper truth and the powers of the spirit world. They *"authenteined"* all the time, in the name of religion.

Their sexual power was combined with a belief system about spirituality and religious power. A dangerous mix. When we know that First Timothy contains this important word which denotes sexual behavior, we see it in a very different light. For example, in the words of a great scholar:

Suppose we were to translate this: 'I forbid a woman to teach or *talk Japanese with a man.'* Then we infer that the injunction applies to the teaching of language. 'I forbid a woman to teach or *dangle a man from the high wire'* would presuppose that the instructor was an aerialist. 'I forbid a woman to teach or *engage in fertility practices* with a man' would imply that the woman should not involve a man in the heretical kind of Christianity which taught licentious behavior as one of its doc-

trines. Such a female heretic did indeed 'teach to fornicate' in the Thyatiran church mentioned in Revelation
2:20.[2]

WHAT WAS FORBIDDEN?

This verse never intended that women stop teaching the
word. It is a prohibition against teaching *licentious doctrine
and behavior.* Similar prohibitions are found in other books
of the New Testament.

> Nevertheless, I have this against you: You tolerate that
> woman Jezebel, who calls herself a prophetess. By her
> teaching she misleads my servants into sexual immorality
> and the eating of food sacrificed to idols. I have given
> her time to repent of her immorality, but she is unwill-
> ing. So I will cast her on a bed of suffering, and I will
> make those who commit adultery with her suffer intense-
> ly, unless they repent of her ways....to you who do not
> hold to her teaching and have not learned Satan's so-
> called deep secrets (I will not impose any other burden
> on you) (Rev. 2:20-24).

Peter described his concern for Christians drawn into this
error.

> But there were also false prophets among the people,
> just as there will be false teachers among you....With
> eyes full of adultery, they never stop sinning; they seduce
> the unstable; they are experts in greed—an accursed
> brood!...For they mouth empty, boastful words and, by
> appealing to the lustful desires of sinful human nature,

they entice people who are just escaping from those who live in error (2 Pet. 2:1,14-18).

GODDESSES AND SATAN

Another church in the same part of the world had a similar problem. The church in Pergamum, like the church in Ephesus, was located in a city where goddess worship prevailed. Satan was revered as a giver of higher enlightenment and deeper truth. To this church, John wrote:

I know where you live—where Satan has his throne. Yet you remain true to my name. You did not renounce your faith in me, even in the days of Antipas, my faithful witness, who was put to death in your city—where Satan lives (Rev. 2:13,14).

AUTHENTEIN: THE STING OF DEATH

The roots of this word go back to a story well known in the gnostic religions of Timothy's day. In this story, fifty virgins were forced to marry men who were their first cousins. They considered this the ultimate bad deal because they believed it a horrendous sin to marry a cousin. All except one murdered the groom on her wedding night. The husband of the exception let her remain a virgin.

Because of this story, writers of Greek drama and love stories used *authentein* when love led to the sting of death or when sex proved fatal, either physically or emotionally. Many of the rites of worship in goddess temples included some enactment, real or pantomimed, of a woman murdering a man. Historians tells us the priestesses of Diana still practiced human sacrifice during the first hundred years after

Christ. Their sacrifices were not beautiful young female virgins, but handsome young virgin men.

We cannot be certain how often this happened, but we do know that when it was not a genuine murder it was a pantomimed one. "The bee priestesses of Artemis (Diana) of Ephesus appear to have delivered a sting of *actual* sex and symbolic death."[3] Common initiation ceremonies in all these religions included a representation of both sex and death.[4]

Paul's choice of *authentein* was no accident. It denoted a misused power well-known to Timothy, a power nearly always associated with religious women, especially those women who *taught* about spiritual matters.

VEXING THE CHURCH FATHERS

These ancient women who *authenteined* were a large part of the reason women were later forbidden to preach. All of us women have, to a degree, been unfairly labeled because of them.

The reaction of church leaders became overreactions as we see in the writings of men like Augustine, Tertullian, and Chrysostom. They were afraid of women having positions in the church where they could again misuse their power.

The *authentein* behavior of the few and their self-given position of "superior spirituality" was so abhorrent to early church leaders that it couldn't help but color attitudes toward all women. It's not surprising these otherwise reasonable men developed negative attitudes toward women and reverted to suppressing their ministry.

Even after the twelve disciples were dead and the church well on its way to adulthood, these kinds of women were still causing problems. A famous church father of that time, Clement of Alexandria, wrote a detailed refutation of the various groups who endorsed fornication as accepted Christian behavior. He complained of those who had turned love-feasts into sex orgies, of those who taught women to "give to every man that asketh of thee," and of those who found physical intercourse as a "mystical communion." He branded one such lewd group *authentai* (the plural of *authentes)*. Then he said, revealing that Christian men were also involved in shameless fornication,

> Others have kicked over the traces and waxed wanton, having become indeed "wild horses who whinny after their neighbors' wives." They have abandoned themselves to lust without restraint and persuade their neighbors to live licentiously.

Continuing, he described them as

> lecherous, incontinent men who fight with their tail, children of darkness and anger, thirsty for their blood, *authentai,* and murderers of their neighbors.[5]

GNOSTICS WERE IN THE GNOW

A group of new Christians gathered in our living room for a Bible study. We were starting at the beginning—the first chapter of Genesis.

"Tonight we'll cover Genesis 1, next week Genesis 2. After that, we'll take three or four chapters each week," explained my husband Jerry.

We never made it past the first two verses. We had a modern gnostic in our midst.

This fellow had recently added Jesus to his bag of religions along with Buddhism, Zoroastrianism, and others.

He became ecstatically happy when we read "God created the heavens."

"Wow! This is great! There's a lot here. Cosmic meaning—like the heavens, you know. That means...and the darkness, that stands for..."

The others listened intently, trying to understand. The moon stood for money, the sun meant eternal life, light stood for something else. He sounded *so deep* and *so spiritual.*

Jerry interrupted, "I'm sorry, brother. That's *not* what it says. It means exactly what it says: God created the heavens and the earth."

"Oh yes, I know. But there are other meanings too—deeper meanings; things of the spirit. We have to look for the deeper truths."

A LONG STRUGGLE

That's a sample of Gnosticism. Knowledge, especially "deep" knowledge, is central, almost worshiped. It comes from the Greek gnosko, to know.

Gnostic beliefs of some type most likely influenced at least half of the Christian believers in the early church.

Christianity was just separating itself from its Jewish ties. The apostles taught, traveled, wrote, and exhorted—working hard to show the difference between faith in Christ and the Jewish religion. Then they had to do the same thing regarding Gnosticism.

Not until the Fourth century A.D. were gnostic ideas labeled heresy and banned officially. It takes a long time to change the way people think, even when those people are born-again Christians and sincerely want to follow God.

Warnings by New Testament writers regarding the errors in various Gnostic beliefs were not only useful to early Christians, we need to hear them today, too.

GNOSIS "CONQUERS MATTER, TIME AND SPACE!"

Just this week, a stack of fliers caught my eye as I waited in a hotel lobby. In huge letters across the top was written "GNOSIS." Below the letters and followed by a mailing address, it said:

GNOSIS is a step-by-step restoration of your native state of being and an elevation beyond that to your optimal existence. The goals of GNOSIS: 1) A restoral of your power of choice in all dynamics of life. 2) To assist you in assuming causes over matter, energy, space and time. 3) To free you from endless incarnations into earthbound physical bodies.

Only those who place their evolutionary progress as spiritual beings should undertake this path. It requires persistence and determination. The reward is total freedom. GNOSIS requires your unbending intent to be the best that you can be. GNOSIS requires that you be willing to observe yourself and the universe around you.

If you desire freedom or seek wisdom, communicate. If you need expanded awareness, self-control, peace of mind, or to conquer your fear, call or write.

TRANCE-LIKE GNOSTICS

Gnosticism wears many labels and appears in a variety of forms. It sometimes appears in our churches or in parachurch Christian groups where a few weird types wander in hoping for some spiritual thrills or mystical revelations.

Some mistaken beliefs about women originated with Gnostic groups. They are an important key to understanding 1 Timothy 2:13: "For Adam was formed first, then Eve."

SPIRITUAL SUPERIORITY

One Gnostic group which troubled the early church was called Quintillianians. They promoted a psuedo-Christian heresy with an intricate theology of the superiority of women. According to the Quintillianians, women had a knowledge of spiritual things *even superior to that of Jesus Christ.* They believed that, starting with Eve, women had an inside track to *gnosis* or secret knowledge and that they had learned more from their prophetesses "than from the law, and prophets, and the Gospels. But they magnify these wretched women above the apostles and every gift of grace, so that some of them presume to assert that there is in them a something superior to Christ."[6]

Another ancient writer, Epiphanius, says that the same group "pretended that the fact of having been the first to eat of the fruit of knowledge (*gnosis*) was for Eve a great privilege."[7]

SECRETS FROM THE SERPENT

Quintillianians were just one of the groups who honored Eve, believing she was the mediator who brought divine enlightenment to mankind. Several groups, known as Ophitic sects (which means honoring the snake), centered their theology on the secret gnosis given to Eve by the serpent "who, they say, gave us the origin of knowledge of good and evil."[8]

Sometimes they gave Eve a prior existence in which she consorted with celestial beings both sexually and intellectually. She was even credited with being the instructor through whom Adam received life.

In one of these myths, Sophia sent Zoe, her daughter, who is called "Eve (of life)," as an instructor to raise up Adam, in whom there was no soul, so that those women he would beget might become vessels of light. When Eve saw her co-likeness cast down, she pitied him, and said, "Adam, live!" Her word became deed. When Adam rose up he immediately opened his eyes. When he saw her, he said, "You will be called 'The Mother of the Living' because you are the one who gave me life." Thus they believed that Eve became the bringer of both light and life.[9]

CORRECTION URGENTLY NEEDED

Paul knew it was important to correct these myths before they were accepted by Christians in Ephesus. In essence he said, "They have it all wrong. Adam was created first rather than Eve. And Eve was not an instrument of light. She was deceived. In her delusion, she believed she would be given knowledge which would make her and Adam like gods."

> For Adam was formed first, then Eve. And Adam was not the one deceived; it was the woman who was deceived and became a sinner (1 Tim. 2:13,14).

Paul wanted them to remember that Adam was not taken in by the serpent's *gnosis*.

"Of course this implies that Adam sinned while knowing perfectly well what he was doing; but this is beside the point of the argument here, which is that Eve was off on the wrong track and that knowledge imparted by Satan is to be shunned by Christians."[10]

ARE WOMEN MORE SPIRITUAL?

Richard and Catharine Kroeger have studied the heresies referred to in First and Second Timothy. Their work supplies valuable knowledge of the place female divinities played in

Greek thinking. And they show *how ancient the superstition is that women are spiritually superior.*

This superstition often appears in Christian circles today, couched in pious-sounding terminology. We often hear (or read), "Women seem to be more sensitive to the Holy Spirit." Or, "Women seem to be closer to God than men." Anytime we allow ourselves to believe this, we are in danger. We are heading the same direction as the Ephesian ladies who were vulnerable to mystical heresies.

THE INTENT OF SCRIPTURE

In a city where the worship of two licentious goddesses permeated daily life, such bizarre sexual/spiritual beliefs could invade the early church.

The Quintillianians, the Ophitics, and other groups like them caused confusion to those outside the church who wondered just what sort of people the Christians were.

Paul's suggestions to the young pastor were practical: Teach the truths of Scripture and don't allow people to believe the old myths and superstitions. Refute old wives tales and stick to the Bible. Preach from Genesis about our origins. Make sure they understand (1) Adam was created first, not second and (2) Eve was thoroughly deceived by Satan, not wisely enlightened by him.

CLEAR DISTINCTION

Christian women in Ephesus were to make a clear distinction between themselves and the temple priestesses and prostitutes. The braids and fashions which identified the servants of Artemis and Aphrodite were not appropriate in that city for Christian women.

Likewise, Christian women were to be willing *learners* in the church, showing a respectful and thoughtful attitude. This

175

attitude set them apart from the pagan religious women and also the heretical Christian groups. Such behavior clearly stated that they did *not* view themselves as spiritually superior or as needing to prove their *(authentein)* control and dominance over men.

ADDENDUM

For the reader who wishes more detail, following is a portion of an article published in the Reformed Journal of March, 1979, and written by Catharine Kroeger from her background of extensive research on the history of the term *authentein* and the heresies which threatened the early church. The article is entitled *Ancient Heresies and a Strange Greek Verb:*

"In Egyptian magic and Gnostic papyri, the term authentes, authentikos, and authentia designated the original, the primordial, the authentic; and by the third century, the concept of the primal source had merged with that of power and authority. In most ancient theologies, creative acts were also sexual ones; and the erotic connotation of authentein lingered on.

"In a lengthy description of various tribes' sexual habits, Michael Glycas, the Byzantine historiographer, uses this verb to describe women who make sexual advances to men and fornicate as much as they please without arousing their husbands' jealousy.

"...But if 1 Timothy 2:12 is understood as a prohibition against promulgating licentious doctrines and practices, how does this tie in with the entire passage? Women are bidden to dress modestly and with propriety (vv. 9-10)—surely a necessity in a city which boasted thousands of prostitutes. Sumptuary laws forbade any but harlots the adornment Paul here proscribes. Imitate not the courtesans, thundered John Chrysostom in his commentary on this passage—and widens his censure to include seductive voice as well as dress. But 'silence' has here to do with receptivity to learning Christian doctrine in subjection to the Gospel.

"In Ephesus, where a great multitude of sacred courtesans

were attached to the shrine of Diana, women had much to unlearn. Previously they had been taught that fornication brought the worshiper into direct communication with the deity. It is worth noting that certain Gnostics and Nestorians employed authentia to indicate a force bringing together the fleshly and the divine. But converts must learn that the one Mediator between God and man was Christ Jesus, and that they must practice their newfound faith in quiet decorum rather than in the wild and clamorous orgies demanded by Ephesian religion.

"The devil had once seduced Eve (the verb in vv. 13 and 14 is also a sexual one) and Jewish tradition held that Satan chose the woman because she was newer and therefore more gullible. She was quite genuinely deceived, supposing that she would gain the knowledge of good and evil and she involved Adam, who was not deceived, in the transgression. To women who had been trained in childhood in the gross immorality of the Phrygian cult, the admonition was certainly appropriate. But prostitutes were active in many areas of ancient life, and some of these found Christ as well.

"Virtually without exception, female teachers among the Greeks were courtesans, such as Aspasia, who numbered Socrates and Pericles among her students. Active in every major school of philosophy, these hetairai made it evident in the course of their lectures that they were available afterwards for a second occupation. But the Bible teaches that to seduce men in such a manner was indeed to lead them to slaughter and the halls of death (cf. Proverbs 2:18; 5:5; 7:27; 9:18). The verb authentein is thus peculiarly apt to describe both the erotic and the murderous."

FOR YOUR OWN BIBLE STUDY

Genesis 1 and 2

Proverbs 2:18; 5:5; 7:27

1 Timothy 2:1-15

2 Peter 2:1-18

Revelation 2:20-24

Chapter 12

Chapter 12

Strength Is for Service

We have been studying and learning about women and our power. God has given us that power so that we can be effective *servants*. This is important. With so much craving for illegitimate power, with so much abuse of the kind of power people use for wrong purposes, we need to clearly understand the Scriptures which show how we are to use our power.

But when we study the passages about serving, some women are likely to take them as encouragement to become servile.

The woman who will react this way is the one who feels she is a victim, not in control of her life. She thinks she has no choice except to go along with the demands of others, to not "rock the boat," and to keep everyone else happy (or at least pacified).

A sadness characterizes this woman, yet she is rarely heard to complain. To onlookers, she appears sweet and saintly. She believes she is doing her Christian duty; she submits. Her burdens are heavy, but she displays a thin smile as she "bears her cross" patiently. Whatever happens, she believes it is probably her fault. She apologizes often, at least once in every conversation.

She hasn't made a choice of her own in so long, she has lost touch with her desires. Given the right to make choices, she has great difficulty: decision-making skills have vanished by long disuse.

She has well-developed skills in waiting on other people, cleaning up after them, picking up their clothes, running their errands, and anticipating their need for a cup of coffee long before it may be requested. This habitual waiting on other people, living as a valet, housemaid, and loyal slave has come to feel normal.

When no one is present to serve, she feels guilty if she does something "selfish" like reading a book or watching TV.

THE VICTIM

This woman has so thoroughly sacrificed herself for others that she has ceased to exist as a separate person. She lives only through her children or husband or whoever it is she serves.

She refuses to allow herself to feel resentment, but that refusal can't last. One day her resentment will erupt like a smoldering fire, and the explosion may be just as surprising to her as to those who took her service for granted all those years.

This woman may *feel* as if she is serving, but she is not. When a person feels victimized, trapped in a situation with no doors opening outward, the normal human reaction is first anger, then depression.

Since many Christians believe anger is a sin, the victim will deliberately command her emotions not to feel anger. Anger turned inward becomes depression. This neat trap is often self-induced by a theology which sounds Christian. It seems spiritual because it emphasizes noble qualities like giving, serving, kindness, thoughtfulness, and self-sacrifice.

Instead of falling into this trap of servility, this woman should recognize the strength she has in Christ, surrender her role as victim, begin to stand up for herself, and take responsibility for her own life and choices.

SERVING IS NOT SERVILITY

A great difference separates Christian service from servility. A woman who knows who she is in Christ can never again be obsequious. She cannot pretend she is a nothing; she knows she is valuable. She has too much self-respect to be trampled, walked on, or treated with disdain. Her life will not be spent as a pawn in someone else's chess game. She does not fall prey to those who dominate by intimidation, temper tantrums, or anger. Her knowledge of her own value prevents her from succumbing to such treatment.

An example is Linda Lovelace Marchiano who wrote of her restoration to self-respect and value in *Out of Bondage*. Once known as the most famous and degraded of all porno stars, she tells of the way she was terrorized by a brutal husband, Chuck Traynor, and forced at gunpoint to submit to the grossest of sexual and violent acts.

Carefully guarded by this cruel macho man who believed

a man's wife was his possession, she rapidly lost her dignity. Chuck wouldn't even let her go to the bathroom alone. He kept a loaded revolver with him at all times and reminded her constantly that if she disobeyed him he would kill not only her, but her family as well.

Few women ever manage to escape this degree of bondage. The fact that Linda escaped is remarkable. Now after more than ten years, she has built a sense of her own value which will prevent her from falling into a life of victimization again.

POWER DELUSIONS

"She is a very powerful person," Mindy once remarked to me.

I wonder what she meant by that comment, I mused later. The lady of whom she spoke had a habit of betraying confidences. Gossip was her favorite sin, usually disguised as concern. ("We really need to pray for Jay and Alice, they're...") My impression of the woman was that she craved power and tended to make herself feel more important by collecting juicy tidbits to share. "Powerful" was not an accurate description. What Mindy actually meant was something like, "That woman scares me! I never know what she may say about me."

In 1983, Tony Campolo, Jr. wrote *The Power Delusion.* His purpose in the book is to reveal power games Christians play, such as husbands who try to gain power over their wives, pastors who try to dominate their church members, and parishioners who try to dominate their pastors. He portrays the religious macho man who has a mistaken view of masculinity. He describes the controlling spiritual leader who uses his charisma to exploit those he leads.

The Power Delusion is good reading for the thoughtful

Christian. It offers a needed balance. Campolo uses the word power, however, as synonymous with coercion. His working definition for the term is "the prerogative to determine what happens and the coercive force to make others yield to your wishes—even against their own will."[1] He believes that the coercive element in power makes it irreconcilable with Christianity.

A BIBLICAL VIEW OF POWER

"Power corrupts and absolute power corrupts absolutely." Every time I hear that statement, it reminds me to be grateful I live in a democracy. Our system of government is far from perfect, but at least it is designed with checks and balances to keep any one leader or group from possessing absolute power. A human being foolish enough to believe he is the last word, the *final* authority, is as frightening as a madman.

When the Bible uses the word power, it is not to indicate coercion or force, but strength. Biblical power is not coercive. It is never power *over* people. It is never given with the right to control others. Knowing we have power doesn't make us arrogant or self-important. It makes us able to meet the needs of others.

During a discussion of status and power, Jesus said, "Whoever wants to become great among you must be your servant, and whoever wants to be first must be slave of all" (Mark 10:43,44). Before Jesus came, power was the opposite of serving. Men of authority were waited on. They never lowered themselves to *be* the servants. It would be too demeaning; serving wouldn't present the correct image.

WORLD-WIDE POWER

Dag Hammarskjold, world statesman, was renowned as a peacemaker among nations. He served for many years as secretary general of the United Nations. His office carried enormous political power and prestige. Possibly more than any living person at that time, he had "clout."

After his death, the manuscript of what is now known as *Markings* was found in his home with a note to his friend that it was primarily a collection of diary entries and, if "you find them worth publishing, you have my permission to do so." Hammarskjold wrote, not for the public, but for himself. His poems and musings were his written "negotiations with myself—and with God."

I am impressed with his genuine humility. He was well aware of the dangers of power and seemed to successfully guard himself against them.

> Around a man who has been pushed into the limelight, a legend begins to grow as it does around a dead man. But a dead man is in no danger of yielding to the temptation to nourish his legend or accept its picture as a reality. I pity the man who falls in love with his image as it is drawn by public opinion during the honeymoon of publicity.[2]

Remembering the arrogance of historical figures who were carried away on the wings of power, he penned, "The shamelessness of great pride; it lifts the crown from the cushion and places it upon its brow with its own hands."[3] This has happened in several instances. The kings involved refused to acknowledge the existence of a higher power than their own will. So when coronation day arrived, they refused to allow any other human to crown them.

SELFISHNESS IS A LONELY LIFE

Dag Hammarskjold also wrote pieces from time to time which showed how much he valued close relationships and desired honest intimacy:

> The overtones are lost, and what is left are conversations which, in their poverty, cannot hide the lack of real contact. We glide past each other. But why? Why _____?

> We reach out towards the other. In vain—because we have never dared to give ourselves.[4]

A more recent writer, Harold Kushner, points out the futility of self-centered living. He writes, not from a Christian point of view, but as a Jewish rabbi, about the person who never feels satisfied in *When All You've Ever Wanted Isn't Enough*. He quotes Ecclesiastes as a description of modern man searching for meaning in all the wrong places and speaks to the loneliness of looking out for number one.

The selfish use of power ends up less than satisfying. People who possess worldly power often don't find this out until it's too late. They're left empty, miserable, and lonely in the empire they have created. But those who understand biblical power do not have that problem. They are fully aware it is a *derived* power, one supplied from a Source outside themselves.

STRENGTH BREEDS GENTLENESS

"It is the weak who are cruel; gentleness is to be expected only from the strong,"[5] said Leo Rosten.

The same could be said for serving. When Jesus wrapped a towel around his waist and began washing his disciples' dusty feet, he was not displaying weakness or a low self-image, but genuine strength. The disciples were embarrassed. They protested. This dirty job was usually done by a slave. It was beneath the dignity of free men.

"Do you understand what I have done for you?" he asked them. "You call me 'Teacher' and 'Lord,' and rightly so, for that is what I am. Now that I, your Lord and Teacher, have washed your feet, you also should wash one another's feet. I have set you an example that you should do as I have done for you. I tell you the truth, no servant is greater than his master, nor is a messenger greater than the one who sent him. Now that you know these things, you will be blessed if you do them" (John 13:12-17).

Jesus didn't feel demeaned in doing the work of a household servant. He had no uneasy ego to protect, no precarious image to maintain. After his resurrection, he appeared to these same disciples one morning when they had taken their boat out on the lake to fish. What was he doing when they spotted him back at the shore? Cooking breakfast.

If we follow Jesus' example, we are in no danger of flying off on a power trip. Jesus had great power, but he chose to see himself as a servant. He told his followers, "For even the Son of Man did not come to be served, but to serve, and to give his life as a ransom for many" (Mark 10:45). That was his life's purpose, and he lived out that purpose daily.

How does this kind of serving differ from the woman we described earlier as the victim? Why is it not servitude or servility? Here's why: Jesus was not a victim. He *chose.* He was not used, manipulated, coerced, or trapped at any point, even in his death. In his discourse on the good shepherd he said, "No one *takes* [my life] from me, but I lay it down of my own accord" (John 10:18). (Italics mine.)

190

CHOOSING TO SERVE

As Christians, we no longer need to live powerlessly. Being a victim is not part of the new life Christ has given us. Why can we say that so confidently? Because Paul's epistle to the Romans deals with that very issue. Romans tells us that powerlessness and the helplessness syndrome was B.C. It's in the past.

"You see, at just the right time, when we *were* still powerless, Christ died for the ungodly" (Rom. 5:6). (Italics mine.)

We used to be powerless. But no more. Christ has solved that problem. Romans 5 makes this announcement: "How much more will those who receive God's abundant provision of grace...*reign in life* through...Jesus Christ" (Rom. 5:17). (Italics mine.) A woman who reigns in life is not a victim—unless she allows herself to be. A woman who reigns in life never says, "I had no choice. There was nothing I could do."

If we are reigning, we *are* making choices. With the power of the Holy Spirit inside us, those choices can be made confidently.

When we choose to use the talents, intelligence, and power God has entrusted to us, we do so not to appease expectations; to get someone off our back; or even worse, to coerce, exploit, and damage others, but to bless them.

This is a more genuine serving than that dutiful drudgery put out by the victim. When we, as free agents—strong, valuable, and empowered by God—cheerfully offer our service to others, it is a true choice. Our service is a gift. No mixed motives. No waiting like the obedient puppy for a pat on the head and a few table scraps.

We love because it is our nature to love. We choose loving

191

service as the best way to live our lives. Living a life of love is the wise choice of a woman who has accepted her God-given power.

FOR YOUR OWN BIBLE STUDY
John 10:18
John 13:12-17
Romans 5:6,17

FOOTNOTES

CHAPTER ONE

[1] Hans Kristian, *Mission Possible* (Bible Voice), p. 59.

[2] Ibid.

CHAPTER FOUR

[1] Thomas A. Harris, MD, *I'm OK, You're OK,* (New York: Harper & Row Publishers, Inc., 1967), p. 254.

[2] For a full theological study of these truths, I recommend: Paul K. Jewett, *Man as Male and Female* (Grand Rapids, MI: Wm. B. Eerdmans Publishing Co., 1975).

CHAPTER SIX

[1] Linda Mercadante, *From Heirarchy to Equality* (Vancouver, B.C. G-M-H Books, 1980), p. 164.

[2] Mercadante, pp. 167-168.

[3] Nathaniel Branden, *The Psychology of Romantic Love* (New York: Bantam Books, Inc., 1980), p. 2.

[4] Ibid., p. 3.

[5] Alan Loy McGinnis, *The Romance Factor* (New York: Harper & Row Publishers, Inc., 1982), p. 97.

CHAPTER NINE

[1] Letty Cottin Pogrebin, *Growing Up Free* (New York: Bantam Books, Inc., 1980), p. 520.

[2] Don Williams, *The Apostle Paul & Women in the Church* (Glendale, CA: Regal Books Division, G/L Publications, 1977), pp. 143-145.
In his book, Don Williams examines each of Paul's letters. He sets each passage on women in its context, showing how it was understood by the believers who first read the letter.
Williams observes:
"Paul is consistent through his letters in bringing women into full equality with men based on the gospel. Thus he *sees* woman's crucial role in God's redemptive purpose through Israel's history which climaxes in the incarnation. Women find their identity in union with Christ, not in marriage and the family. Thus Paul commends both celibacy and marriage as vehicles for their discipleship. Further-

more, Paul is free from sexual stereotypes and polarization."

This writer demonstrates that Paul not only wrote the famous Christian Magna Charta but lived out its implications in his ministry and preaching. (Neither Jew nor Greek, slave nor free, male nor female).

"Since we are now all one in Christ Jesus, this must mean one in ministry. The gifts of the Holy Spirit are never given with preference to the male. We live in...the power of the Holy Spirit, [who] is shattering the old expectations and molds. Women are now exercising gifts of ministry by praying and prophesying (1 Cor. 11:5). Not only this, they are being "ordained" for ministry as well. Phoebe is a "deacon" (Rom. 16:1,2). Prisca, Euodia, and Syntyche are "fellow workers," standing side by side with men such as Aquila and Clement (Rom. 16:3; Phil. 4:2,3). The office of deacon is to be filled by women who are "serious, not slanderers, but temperate, faithful in ministry" (1 Tim. 3:2). Widows are to be enrolled for special ministry (1 Tim. 5:3) and older women are to teach younger women their domestic duties (Titus 2:3-5).

"The sharing of women in ministry calls forth the strongest affirmation from Paul. Phoebe has been a helper of the Apostle (Rom. 16:2). Prisca joined Aquila in risking her neck for Paul and all the churches are thankful for her (Rom. 16:3,4). Mary worked hard among the Romans (Rom. 16:6). Rufus' mother mothered Paul (Rom. 16:13). Nymphas has a church in her house (Col. 4:15). Chloe's people report to Paul (1 Cor. 1:11). Lois and Eunice have a sincere faith (2 Tim. 1:5), and Apphia is a sister in the Lord to Paul and Timothy (Phil. 2). It is exactly in the incidental nature of these references that makes them all the more impressive. Paul loved, affirmed, depended upon, and ministered with women. They in turn found a new identity and new roles both in Christ and in the Christian community. Catapulted beyond domesticity, women now carry out a full range of gifted functions, spreading the gospel and building up the church."

[3] Dorothy Sayers, *Are Women Human?* (Grand Rapids, MI: Wm. B. Eerdmans Publishing Co., 1971), p. 47.

[4] F.F. Bruce, *Bruce Commentary on Galatians* (Grand Rapids, MI: Wm. B. Eerdmans Publishing Co., 1982), p. 190.

Dr. F.F. Bruce is one of many thoughtful scholars who points out

196

Paul's emphasis on equality: "No more restriction is implied in Paul's equalizing of the status of male and female in Christ than in his equalizing of the status of Jews and Gentiles, or of slave and-free person. If in ordinary life, existence in Christ is manifested openly in church fellowship, then if a Gentile may exercise spiritual leadership in the church as freely as a Jew, or a slave as freely as a citizen, why not a woman as freely as a man?

"Paul states the basic principle in Galatians 3:28. If restrictions on it are found elsewhere in the Pauline epistles such as in 1 Corinthians 14:34 or 1 Timothy 2:11 they are to be understood in relation to Galatians 3:28 and not vice versa."

CHAPTER TEN

[1] Richard and Catharine Kroeger, "May Women Teach? Heresy in the Pastoral Epistles," *The Reformed Journal* (Grand Rapids, MI: Wm. B. Eerdmans Publishing Co., Oct. 1980), pp. 15-16. (Used by permission)

CHAPTER ELEVEN

[1] Jessie Penn-Lewis, *The Magna Charta of Women* (Minneapolis, MN: Bethany Fellowship, Inc., 1975), pp. 9,10.

[2] Catharine Kroeger, "Ancient Heresies and a Strange Greek Verb," *The Reformed Journal* (Grand Rapids, MI: Wm. B. Eerdmans Publishing Co., October 1979), p. 14. (Used by permission)

[3] Richard and Catharine Kroeger, "May Women Teach? Heresy in the Pastoral Epistles," *The Reformed Journal* (Grand Rapids, MI: Wm. B. Eerdmans Publishing Co., October 1980), p. 17. (Used by permission)

[4] Ibid., p. 17.

[5] Catharine Kroeger, "Ancient Heresies and a Strange Greek Verb," *The Reformed Journal* (Grand Rapids, MI: Wm. B. Eerdmans Publishing Co., March 1979), p. 14. (Used by permission)

[6] Richard and Catharine Kroeger, "May Women Teach? Heresy in the Pastoral Epistles," *The Reformed Journal* (Grand Rapids, MI: Wm. B. Eerdmans Publishing Co., October 1980), p. 16. (Used by permission)

[7] Ibid., p. 16.
[8] Ibid.
[9] Ibid., pp. 16,17.
[10] Ibid.

CHAPTER TWELVE

[1] Anthony Campolo, Jr., *The Power Delusion* (Wheaton, IL: Victor Books a division of SP Publications, Inc., 1983), p. 11.
[2] Dag Hammarskjold, *Markings* trans. Leif Sjorberg and W.H. Auden, (New York: Alfred A. Knopf, 1965), p. 66.
[3] Ibid., p. 164.
[4] Ibid., p. 40.
[5] Leo Rosten, quoted by Leo Buscaglia in *Living, Loving and Learning* (New York: Fawcett Columbine: Published by Ballantine Books, 1982), Steven Short, p. 37.